TEACHER
ON THE
HIGH
WIRE

MARJORIE
RADCLIFFE

Marjorie K. Radcliffe

CHAPTER ORDER

1. Farewell to Teaching   5
2. The Education of a Traveling Tutor   11
3. I Join the Circus   17
4. First Days   23
5. Settling In   29
6. School   35
7. Load-in and Set-up   43
8. Load-out   49
9. The Grand Circle Tour   55
10 On the Rails   63
11. The Cold   67
12. Downtime   73
13. Death in the Circus   79
14. Gunther   83
15. Circus Gossip   89
16. Arizona   95
17. Mugged in Mexico   101
18. The Buffalo Act   105
19. The Chinese   111
20. The Big Cats   115
21. The Baboons   121
22. The Elephants   125
23. The Clown   131
24. The Chicago Kidz   135
25. Goodbye to the Circus   141

CHAPTER 1

FAREWELL TO TEACHING

It finally happened. I lost my job. It wasn't much of a job, but I had lost so much in recent years that this felt like the final straw. In the past year, I had divorced, my children had both left for University, and my waterfront home was on the market. My supposed country club friends now talked about me, rather than to me. I was forty-eight years old and an object of pity. I knew that if I stuck around my old haunts, I would have constant reminders of my previous life. I might bump into my doctor ex-husband and his girlfriend without warning. I couldn't face that humiliation.

There was only one solution. I had to get away from the scene of the crime and move to a new city. I chose a mid-Florida town where I had family. I moved in with my sister for a while, before I started looking for a house, a home where my children could visit. It was a new experience for me, choosing a house, choosing furniture. After years of being a pleaser, I didn't know my own taste. Still, I got there. I settled in and tackled the next challenge: finding a job.

Jumping into the job market after twenty-five years of being a secondary earner and a homemaker was frightening. I found a position as a Spanish teacher at a local high school. The fact that I was the fourth teacher in the position in four years should have told me something. The assistant principal who hired me enjoyed the power of hiring and firing.

Then, whoever selected the students for each class had dumped me with some prime misfits. When I tried to interest a counselor in my problem, he just leaned over his desk and said, "You mean you can't handle it Mrs. R? Is that what you are telling me? You can't handle it?" Damn right, I couldn't handle it!

For the next school year, I taught first-year Spanish to large classes of aspiring delinquents. These kids chewed me up and spat me out daily, and, even though I had no other job prospects, the idea of unemployment came as a relief. My worst class was second period. A couple of bullies, Kevin and George, dominated the other students. Everyone feared them – including me! When I turned to write on the chalk board, pennies hit the back of my head and neck. Nobody dared say who was doing it, but it was obvious. Every lesson was a battle and I lost on a regular basis.

One day, I reached the end of my rope. "You are packing for a trip," I said. "What do you put in the case?" "*¿Qué pones en la maleta?*" I asked continually. We had been learning articles of clothing, and from most students I would get some kind of a response: "*una camisa, un vestido, un traje de baño*": a shirt, a dress, a bathing suit. Finally I came to George.

"*Oye, Jorge,*" I said. "*¿Qué pones en la maleta?*" After a painful pause he came up with "*Una camisa.*"

"*¿Qué más? ¿Qué más?*" What more, what more? I urged. I could see the wheels turning, but he was getting nowhere. Finally his expression turned crafty.

He leaned back, fixed me with a grin and said, "How do you say jock strap in Spanish Mrs. R?"

The class erupted. What could I do? I threw caution to the wind. "Don't worry about it, Jorge," I said. "You don't need one."

The students started chalking imaginary scores on an imaginary board. "Score one for Mrs. R," someone yelled.

That's one of my major faults. Sometimes I only open my mouth to change feet. I got a cheap laugh, but I knew I was going to pay for it.

I realized that I was also in a class war. Despite years in the States, I still had an English accent. This might be considered attractive by some,

6

but to a few of the proletariat kids in my classes it was a cry to bring out the tumbrels and start sharpening the guillotine. The revolutionary spirit reigned in this part of Florida. Then again, the motivation may have just been the American desire for equality. These students preferred people closer to their own level. I didn't make that cut, so they set out to make my life a misery. It wasn't only me though. They had other victims.

One of my students was a classy young woman from an affluent background. She sometimes arrived late to class, since she was seeing a psychiatrist on a regular basis. Twice a week, when she entered the classroom the bullies would start in on her. "Here comes Psycho," they would say. "How did it go, Psycho?"

She would sit down, pull out her books and try to ignore them, but I knew that she suffered, that the constant taunts were getting to her. One day, on a group field trip, when I was sitting apart from the rest, she came to sit with me. She told me her story. She had been attending a private school where one of the boys in her group had told her that he was going to commit suicide. He said that the only thing that would stop this would be if she had sex with him.

"Mrs. R, I am a virgin," she said. "I couldn't do it. I didn't think he was serious anyway. Well, he went off and killed himself. I cracked! My parents pulled me out of that school and I came here. I feel so bad!'

What could I as a teacher do? What advice could I give? I gave it some thought. "Hey, don't beat yourself up," I said. "He was going to kill himself, no matter what you did. He was looking to grab some goodies on the way out. He probably pitched that same argument to some of the other girls. Think how you would have felt if you did come through and he still killed himself? You'd have spent the rest of your life thinking you were a lousy lay." She laughed, but maybe it's a good thing I didn't go into counseling.

There was such a bad atmosphere in that school, and the teachers took all the heat. Administration closed ranks. They sided with the students and parents. They even spied on us. My staffroom had two-way radio, and all our conversations were overheard by head office. The teachers were cannon fodder. One day, in class a couple of the bullies started in with the usual play threats.

"What kind of a car do you drive, Mrs. R?" someone asked.

One of the other teachers had sugar poured into her gas tank. This kid was telling me and the rest of the class that he could sabotage my car any time he wanted.

No problem, I thought. "It's a grey Porsche," I answered. "It's parked right in front of the school." That was the principal's car. I figured that he'd fostered this climate, so he could take the heat.

Anyway, at the end of that horrific year of confrontational teaching, I was informed that my services were no longer required. I'd been fired, or "let go" as some like to call it.

I so much prefer being let go to being fired. When you are let go, it sounds as if you were straining to get away. Your employer was trying to hold you back, but you prevailed. You slipped the leash and escaped. When you are fired, it's quite different. They drop you into the mouth of a cannon and light the fuse. They can't get rid of you fast enough. But I had been let go.

I went home that final day and took to my bed, vowing that I would sell this aging body on the streets rather than go through that again. My career as a high school Spanish teacher was over. I bought a sack of used Harlequin romances and submerged myself in fiction where a handsome hero with burning glances and a six-pack (I mean abs, not beer) saves the day. I might never work again, or, at least, I might never work in education. I had been a chemistry/math teacher in England. I had taught PE at a convent. I'd owned my own business: a book shop. In this country, I had acquired a B.A. in French and was Phi Beta Kappa. I also had an M.A. in Spanish, but I still felt like a failure.

My self-imposed retirement lasted for a few weeks until one day, reading the local classifieds, I noticed an advertisement looking for tutors to teach at Universal or Disney. A New York company had contracts to provide tutors to the local entertainment businesses. Young actors in movies, commercials, and so on have to keep up with their studies and sometimes this means having a tutor involved.

I telephoned and set up an interview. The next day, I rolled out of bed, showered, and for the first time in days, put on some business clothes and makeup. My interview took place in a hotel room near Universal Drive. My interviewer was a hyper young guy from New York City. He owned the company and he was all business.

What could I do? What could I teach? That was easy. "Everything," I said. "Well, everything except ROTC and shop." That was the right answer. He hired me on the spot.

CHAPTER 2

THE EDUCATION OF A TRAVELING TUTOR

My first jobs as a tutor involved teaching odd hours in various locations near or at Universal Studios or Disney. One of the most memorable kids was an ex-Mouseketeer: a redhead with designs shaved into his scalp. He was typical of the kids who get into acting. He wanted attention. He wanted to be noticed. He was also a bright kid, which after my last experience was quite a plus. I made very little money. It was just a couple of hours here and there but I was paying my dues and showing that I was a capable teacher who could get along with students on an individual basis without fighting urges to kill or sexually abuse them. Soon I would be ready for the big time.

Eventually I graduated. I passed the test and was judged ready to go on the road. The company offered me a job traveling around the United States with a show called *The Playboy of the Western World*. A group of Irish actors from Dublin had just started this tour.

Dublin has two outstanding theaters: the Gate Theatre, which concentrates on Ibsen, Shakespeare, and so on, and the Abbey Theatre, which deals mainly with stories about the common people – the peasants. The Gate has a lot of gay actors while the Abbey's actors are mainly straight. The locals refer to these theaters as Sodom and Begorrah. The Gate was

Sodom, and the Abbey was Begorrah. *Playboy*, performed by actors from the Abbey, was opening in Washington, D.C. at the Kennedy Center. I was to fly up there and be the traveling tutor, responsible for the education of one thirteen-year-old-boy, Eoin, the child of Nula, the principal actress.

As soon as I arrived in town, I was given a ticket to a performance and that evening I watched the play. It tells the story of a young man who claims to have killed his Da (that's father for those of you unfamiliar with the Irish vernacular). What an experience! The Abbey specializes in stories about the common people. Well, the common people evidently had broad Irish accents and vocabularies to match. Furthermore, all the actors were dressed in rags and had dirty bare feet. I and the rest of the audience were stunned to realize that we had come to watch a play in a foreign language.

"The Peelers be comin'," meant "The Police are on their way." (Robert Peel started the British police force, hence they are called Bobbies in England and Peelers in Ireland.) You'd think that with my English background I would have little difficulty following the dialogue. You'd be wrong. I was mystified. I had to watch the play several times before I fully understood what was happening. Still, the American public is very tolerant and figured that they must be absorbing culture.

My student, Eoin, was a great kid. I taught him algebra, French, and core subjects, but a member of the cast helped him with Gaelic. This still left me plenty of time to socialize and enjoy the various cities. Washington, D.C. was my favorite city. It was an education for us all. The Irish wielded considerable power in the U.S. government, and one insider, a banker, was very good to us. He knew many of the movers and shakers, so he was able to escort Eoin, his mother, Nula, and myself around the centers of government. This banker's ancestors came from the Old Country and he was determined to show his fellow countrymen a good time while they were here. He told us that, when the show came to Minneapolis/St. Paul, he would throw a party for the whole cast. That turned out to be quite an experience. It was interesting to be part of a group who were feted for their nationality. The Irish stick together. In every city, the Irish would turn out to show us around. I remember a local priest taking us out to the Irish pub after one show and confessing (in his beer) that he had broken all his vows – except poverty!

We usually traveled by bus or plane. It was an education for me to realize just how cultured was this group of actors who would bury themselves in books such as *The Life of Garcia Lorca* and discuss poetry and literature with such enthusiasm. They also drank with enthusiasm. I figured that many of the cast were either alcoholics or recovering alcoholics. One of the actors, David, whom I still see quite often in movie character parts, would have breakfast with me regularly. I was an early riser and he, his liver having been "distryed by the drink," would be driven from his bed at the crack of dawn by pangs of hunger, and have to refuel. He would shake his head mournfully as he recounted the tragedy of his drinking problems.

"I niver did like drunks, Midarlin," he confessed, "even when I wuz one."

I loved those early morning breakfasts when David would tell me stories of the people he had known through the years. He told me about Picasso standing on a beach in France as the waves swept in and turned the sand into a wet pallet. The artist knelt down and quickly sketched something into the sand with his finger. He just had time to sign it before the next wave came in and erased it all. A treasure lost! David said that Picasso's cleaning lady never cashed his checks, because his signature on the checks was worth more than the amount she was paid. He told me about the poet, Robert Graves, being buried in Majorca, how the mourners had concrete poured over the grave site, and had written the dates of birth and death in the wet mixture. "They placed no headstone," he said, "because they did not want to impede the flow of the spirit!" What poetic wonderful words!

When we flew into Lincoln, Nebraska, I sat next to a psychologist. He commented on the accents of the people in my group and we began to talk. He told me that he worked for Gallup and specialized in placing people in business where they would be most productive and happy. "Happiness," he said, "is hard to pinpoint. People can always tell you why they are unhappy in their work, but when they are happy and productive, they can't tell you why. That's what I figure out." He interviewed people who worked in research, sales, or administration, then moved them about in a company until their abilities matched their position.

"If you were a quiet, introverted person and you wanted to be a sergeant major," he said, "I could train you to do the job by the book, but at best you would be mediocre. To do a job well, it's not enough to have the education and training to match the position. All your natural responses must be appropriate to the needs of the job. You must do it well, but without effort." I liked that answer. I figured I was finally in the right line of work.

Eventually, toward the end of the tour, we arrived in Minneapolis and were invited by our D.C. banker to the promised welcome party. We were picked up at the theater door in a collection of cars: three-year-old Chryslers and Chevys that would attract no interest in any normal neighborhood. We were driven to the outskirts of the city. The house belonging to our host was on no city street and had no sign or number indicating its location or owner. Our driver peeled through a gap in a ragged hedgerow, drove across a field, slipped through another gap, across a second field and there stood the house. It was a large building that had been added to through the years as the family grew. Inside it was comfortably furnished with solid quality pieces, built to last. Waitresses circulated with appetizers and drinks, not the cheap wine, cheese and crackers of the usual large-scale bash, but quality wines, pâté, and lobster. We were in the home of one of the "Out- of- Sight Rich."

I had lived several years before in a Florida town famous for the quality of its real estate. The *nouveau riche* who lived there liked to flaunt their wealth. New Mercedes and BMWs decorated the front drives of their multimillion-dollar mansions. The out-of-sight rich play a different game. They prefer to keep a low profile. Their wealth is hidden so that it does not attract the attention of potential kidnappers or the IRS. Discretion is the word!

For a low-profile town, however, Minneapolis has a high-profile mall. Minneapolis/St. Paul is famous for its megamall, "The Mall of America," a truly amazing place. For the power shopper it is heaven on earth, and for those retail junkies who have passed on to their reward, it is just heaven. When I die, I plan to have my ashes scattered there so that I can shop for eternity.

Eventually the tour came to an end. I returned to suburbia, feeling that all the excitement had gone out of my life. That's when I got the call about my next gig. What a change of pace! I had been sold to the circus!

CHAPTER 3

I JOIN THE CIRCUS

"How do you feel about a job working for a circus? Do you want to try out for a position as the teacher for Ringling Brothers?"

Wow! Megawow! I was about to run away with the circus. I, a very proper fifty-year-old lady from academia, was about to break the mold. It's something that most of us can never do: pick up and leave behind all we have worked for – home, friends, children, and husband. I was in a unique position, however. I had divorced three years earlier and moved to a new city. I had no romantic attachments. My two children had just finished their education and started their working careers. They both moved into my new home in Winter Park, Florida. After all, as far as they were concerned, living with me was great. The price was right, and the service was pretty good. I could be doing their laundry and buying their groceries for the rest of my life. I finally figured out a solution. If your children won't leave home, you have to! I had few friends in this new location, and my house? I could just walk away and leave them to it.

I traveled up to New York City and checked into a hotel near Madison Square Garden. The circus generally performs at the Garden for a couple of months in the first year of its two-year tour. This was in the old days before Mayor Giuliani cleaned up the place. At that time it was the big, bad city with mean, angry misfits preaching on street corners, and drunks and druggies hanging about in the subways. Just getting across the road to the Garden was a challenge. Anyway, I made it there and had my first experience with head office, circus style. There I met Tim.

Tim, the unit manager who interviewed me, was a tall, nice-looking young man. I say young, since from the point of view of a fifty-year-old, thirty is definitely young. Tim had joined the circus when he was still a kid. He had learned the ropes: how everything worked and tied together, both on the circus train and in the arenas where the circus performed. The circus has three basic crews of workers: animal crew, building crew, and train crew. When Tim first joined the circus, he worked with the animal crew. He spread straw, groomed horses, and shoveled elephant excrement. Then he moved to the building crew, working backstage and the ring. Later, he switched to the train crew and became an engineer, then circus trainmaster. Now he was General Manager of the Red Unit.

I had come to apply for the job as circus schoolteacher, but I think we interviewed each other. He was soft-spoken and self-taught. His grammar and diction were excellent, in spite of his constant exposure to poor speech. When I first met him I thought he was an Ivy League Business School graduate. Only the tattoo I caught sight of under the sleeve of his shirt hinted that he had not come from the normal business world. He's the kind of American who made this country great: always thirsting for knowledge and willing to work hard to get ahead.

Tim's history fascinated me. He was impressive. He had done it all. At thirty he had an incredible depth of experience. I think he said he was fourteen when he started taking care of the animals. Of course, he had lied about his age. I never learned what drove him to go out on his own so young, but he had made good. I liked him. Anyway, he must have liked me too. I remember Tim questioning me.

"Why does someone like you want to work for the circus? I've looked at your résumé. It's not your usual type of job."

"Life experience," was my answer. I still feel that way when I come across something new and exciting. It doesn't have to be upscale or comfortable. It just has to be stimulating and different. He must have understood where I was coming from. He hired me!

I flew back home to Florida and spent the next weeks organizing my move. In May of 1991, I flew into Bradley Airport, outside Hartford, Connecticut, to join up with the Red Unit. Mark, a lively, dark-haired young man from Tucson, met me as I left the plane. Mark had started with Ringling as a cook. Now he was the purchasing agent for the train. He drove a Grand Prix, which was carried on the flats between cities. Mark collected my luggage and drove me to the railroad yards. Here I had my first view of the train: a long procession of silver-painted coaches with the red RBB&B logos stretched along them, and a tail-end procession of flats: long parallel metal beams upon which vehicles can be carried.

He parked the car near one of the coach vestibules and helped me haul my stuff aboard coach number 57. Maneuvering out of his car and staggering across dirt and hunks of granite in my narrow, wedged, open-toe shoes was no picnic. My business suit and nylon panty hose didn't help either. I felt clumsy and out of place. As we clambered up the high steps leading to the vestibule, Mark pointed out the garbage bags tied to the hand rails. This was where trash was deposited. Down the narrow corridor we came to my room. Room 5 was called a double. It had a sink and refrigerator at one end and a shower and clothes closet at the other. The long inside wall against the corridor had my bunk. This was a wooden shell, bolted to the wall, with a thick foam pad sitting in the hollow. It could be folded flat against the wall, but what need? There was no extra furniture to put in the space, so it stayed down all day. The outside wall had two long picture windows and a narrow Formica desk top. There were half a dozen of these double rooms in my coach, separated in the middle by two "donnikers." These donnikers are the train version of a toilet. They have holding tanks underneath the coach and have to be emptied periodically. I remember, in one city, seeing a truck arrive at the train to pump them out. I was in shock! Painted on the side of the truck were the words "Your Shit Is My Bread and Butter."

I soon parked my luggage then went out shopping with Mark. We went to a nearby Price Club to pick up supplies. I bought a microwave, a cooking ring and a collection of pans. That evening I ate at the mall with Mark, but the following day I was introduced to dining, circus style. I ate at the Pie Car. The Pie Car is a circus icon, a train car converted into something like a diner. It is the place where the circus workers eat. It is the heart and soul of the train and the pipeline to all the latest gossip. The cooks turned out the specials of the day, plus the usual burgers, sandwiches, and coffee. The performers usually had their own cooking facilities in their rooms, so the majority of the Pie Car diners were the train crew, the vehicle drivers, and the animal crew.

The first few nights on the circus train took some adjusting. When performing in a city, the train will sit on the tracks. The only disturbance came from the voices in the corridor outside.

"What time's the first show?"

"Hey, did you see the animal rights crazies outside the building?"

Someone had left sheets and pillow cases in my room, so I made up the bed, unpacked my clothes and settled in for the night. Still, the AC was blasting from the roof vent and I almost froze in bed. A previous occupant had already tried to plug the vent with fiberglass, but without success. For the next few nights I wore a sweatshirt and a warm nightie, and I lay under a quilt with my bed socks poking out. Eventually Tim loaned me a heater. I figured I could also use a TV, a radio, and a CD player. I was assembling a long list of essentials.

It's not easy to acquire the necessities of day-to-day living when the shops are too far or the journey too dangerous to attempt. The train is often parked off in the boonies: Nowheresville, where you need a taxi to get to a phone booth to call a taxi. Sometimes we would be on the mean streets of downtown, opposite the crack houses. Once a week, the circus bus took the train crew – and now me – to the Laundromat and the grocery store. Generally the guys put their laundry in the machines and retired to a local bar while I shopped for food. The men who lived in the bunk car didn't buy food since they had no place to secure it. Still, they were good to me, carrying my groceries back to my coach on the train and giving me a helpful push on my rear end as I struggled to climb onto the high step of the vestibule. What gentlemen!

CHAPTER 4

FIRST DAYS

I awoke early, that first day on the circus train. There were no drapes or blinds, so bright sunlight shone through the length of my windows. At least, I didn't have to worry about Peeping Toms. We were too high above the trackside for that. I could stumble to my shower without embarrassment. Water splashed on my carpet. Soon I would need to add a plastic shower curtain so that I didn't drench everything. A quick change into my schoolteacher outfit and it was off to the Pie Car for breakfast. Clambering down the steps from the vestibule of 57 coach to the heavy yellow stool below was a major gymnastic feat. It stretched my joints and my pantyhose to the limit. Then I stumbled over the trackside rubble to the Pie Car for breakfast and more gymnastics to get aboard again. I filed down the short corridor to the counter.

The cook stared at me. "You the new teacher?" he asked.

The Pie Car is the gossip mill, the news center for the whole circus, and I was today's news. Several eaters turned around to stare at me.

I was taken aback. "Yes," I admitted warily.

He broke into a smile. "Hey, good to meet you, Teach. My name's Jim. What'll you have then?"

"I'm Marjorie," I said, hastily scanning the menu, "and I'll have an egg sandwich and a coffee, please."

I paid and carried my food to one of the booths, where I ate slowly and watched the comings and goings of the circus guys. The customers were mainly men, and morning was obviously a busy time for the Pie Car. I stayed silent and waited for my bus, a long silver replica of the circus train with the red stripe bearing white letters that proclaimed Ringling was in town.

At 9:30, this was the last bus to the arena. It crawled alongside the train, picking up stragglers, then bumped over the train tracks and out of the yard onto the streets. When we got to our destination, the big downtown arena, we passed through a parking area crammed with trailers, wagons, trucks, mobile homes, and cars. Just outside the large, cavernous entrance to the building was the Pie Car Junior, a small wagon that is towed to the arena in every city. At every venue it is parked just inside the building or near the entrance. Here circus employees buy their food. The cooks, Gary and Ernie, were flipping burgers and making fried egg sandwiches for the early morning circus crowd. The bus driver, wearing a jacket with the RBB&B Circus logo, was flashing various checks for a mixture of wages and piece work he'd earned on the flats and the frame.

I stopped by 14 wagon, the mobile administration office. Tim was busy and I wasn't scheduled to teach yet, so I just checked to see if my stuff had arrived. The boxes of books I'd mailed ahead were not in evidence so I looked at the supplies already in the school box and headed into the building. Willie, the temporary teacher, was busy. She was going to finish up the week, so I just introduced myself and headed off to the mall. From there, I made it back to the building in time to get the last bus back to the train and dinner in the Pie Car. Here, the circus gossips were busy.

"Hey, I hear our driver might be leaving soon. He's just had another accident and scraped the mirror off the bus again."

"Better than scraping something off one of us!" offered another.

"Yeah, like an arm or a leg," came the reply. "I hear the dismemberment policy is just $10,000 a limb and half pay."

Wow! The guys were on a run, trying to impress the newcomers, or just trying to scare them. One of them came over and sat opposite me.

"You're the new teacher, aren't you? Can you teach me to read?" I was taken aback.

"I'm sorry. I don't know what my duties will be yet. I think I'm just here for the children."

"Well, you'd better leave now then, before the building crew gets here. Those guys talk real dirty. I'm OK because you remind me of my mother. Can I bring you a rose tomorrow?"

Cases of beer were arriving and the noise level was rising. I decided to take his advice and go. I said no to the rose. He probably hated his mother anyway. I didn't like his body language: his face was too close and menacing. I planned to stay away from the Pie Car when he was around.

The following day, our last day in Hartford, I took the first bus and arrived at the building early. I soon learned what I could expect in the days ahead. I walked in past a row of chained elephants and a quantity of horses – some chestnut, some white. The elephants were huge beasts, constantly swaying from side to side, their trunks lolling. There were twenty-one of them, mostly female, a long ponderous row of grey wrinkled leather. The size and quantity of a herd of elephants is awesome, but at first they seemed like dull-witted bulks. The only stand-out was Congo, an African elephant with enormous ears and huge tusks capped in silver. In comparison to the elephants, the horses with their early morning erections seemed vital and energetic with groomed bodies of close dense hair. Tall plumes of turquoise feathers would be added when they were about to go into the ring.

The elephant herd, the horses, and the big cats: all these belonged to the circus. These were permanent. They had their place on the circus train and were hauled with us from city to city. Other animals belonged to individual owners who provided them as part of a two-year contract. The owners transported these in their own trucks and personally cared for them. At different times there were miniature ponies, buffalo, zebras, long-horns, dogs, llamas, baboons, camels, chimpanzees and, before my time, bears and even an alligator. The tigers were a breed apart though. They paced about in their holding cages, ignoring the larger adults who passed by, but came alive when a small child or a dog came close, tracking them with their eyes, their instincts kicking in. Small animals mean easy prey.

Beyond the livestock and through the back corridors of the arena were the dressing areas: curtained sections smelling of sweat and talcum powder. Clowns with large painted smiles and frowns, glittering teardrops, and rainbow mops of hair bustled in the passageways. Clowns spend a lot of time at the building. They are used extensively for promotion. They know how to act perennially upbeat, always giving a positive slant to the circus news. Other people may turn sour from time to time, but never the clowns.

Eventually I found the school area and finally came across the boxes of teaching materials that I had mailed ahead. I never knew where I would be teaching in each building. Willie, the temporary teacher, was to have class that day in the front restaurant bar. After a quick look around, I went with Mark across the arena to see her. Willie filled me in with some information about students and parents. Later, John, the Performance Director, led me to a place in the audience where I watched my first show. There was an amazing succession of acts where performers and animals melded together in an incredible confusion of movement and color. My senses were overwhelmed. Then, when I made my way down to the exit, I passed through a gauntlet of tigers, elephants, horses, zebras, dogs, and ponies.

These animals were to become a large part of my life. Their presence, their smell was overwhelming. Would the animal perspiration become part of my aroma too? Would I smell of animals? I remember that in England, where I was born, the owners of fish-and-chip shops used to reek of frying oil. It condensed on their skin, hair, and clothing. Now I am blessed with a poor sense of smell, but when an elephant passed wind near me I could certainly smell it. I mentioned this later, on the bus back to the train. One of the animal crew told me about sitting next to a lady on a public bus. She sniffed toward him and said, "I can smell elephants." He'd been wearing clean clothing, but earlier that day, he'd been paid $75 for cleaning out the elephant car.

"That elephant crap was sticking to my shoes," he said. "I should have noticed it. Elephant crap is heavy stuff. Now, horse crap? That's dryer. It's lighter. Cleaning a horse stall is an easier job. That's why they pay more for cleaning out the elephant car. Sometimes that crap is so heavy sticking to my shoes that I can hardly walk."

Back at the train, I saw Mark again. We went off to the local Price Club to pick up more supplies. This time I bought a crock pot, cooking utensils, and dishes. In the evening, Willie drove by the train and I went out with her to eat at the Mall. Later, when I was back in my room, she came by with her daughter to say goodbye. The daughter was thrilled. She had been allowed to lead a Shetland pony and walk from the arena to the train in the animal parade. When they left, I prepared for bed, shivering as I snuggled under the covers. I piled on the clothes and lay under the quilt, my bed socks poking out. My stomach itched intensely. Had I caught a flea already?

It takes a long time to load out from a building. That night, I went to bed before midnight. I felt the first lurches of the train at 2:40, but it didn't start moving properly until 7:00 a.m. We slid out past the rusting debris of the city outskirts, then past lakes, trees, and warehouses and finally, at 11:00 a.m., we were there. We had reached Springfield, Massachusetts. I had done my first circus move.

With a whole day left to use up, I walked to the West Springfield shops with Rick, one of the animal crew. Rick helped carry my groceries. "Hey, you don't ever need to buy carrots." he informed me. "I can get you a 30 pound bag any day. The elephants will be happy to share." He hauled the bags onto my coach, saw my room, and was envious. He shared a room with another man and used communal showers. His shoulder was aching. He'd been struck in the shower the previous day by a troublemaker who subsequently got fired. It's a rough life for the men, living in close quarters with the aggressive types who come and go.

Rick was hoping that his new girlfriend, someone he met in New York, would come to spend time with him, maybe even try out for the show. "She's going to audition to be a dancer," he told me, proudly producing a picture. She was just a body in a swimsuit, and I mean, just a body! To get the important stuff in the picture he had left off the head. "She's going to see if she can dance well enough to wear the tinsel." A couple stopped us to ask when the animals would unload. "Not till tomorrow morning," said Rick, hurrying off to buy cards to send to New York. Ah, long-distance love and lonely men!

CHAPTER 5

SETTLING IN

There is a lot to learn during the first year of circus living. I spent some time working on the schedules. I had to get out early every morning to see if the bus times were posted in the Pie Car. Getting there was always an ordeal. The sides of the track are usually scattered with rough chunks of stone. It's hard on the ankles. Still, things were better after I bought some casual clothes and sensible shoes. What a change! I started to wear pants and T-shirts. I ordered a circus jacket with Teach embroidered on the front. My new persona was far more pleasurable and comfortable than the old me. Inside and out, I was changing and was acquiring a new and more colorful vocabulary. Not for the classroom, however.

Once we arrived in a new town, the day-to-day organization started. Recently, the train had been parked parallel to a narrow two-way street alongside the track. In the morning I walked toward the oncoming traffic to get to the early bus. The venders had to be at the building at least two hours before a show, and on the first day I usually traveled with them. We were always on our toes, anxious to see if the animal rights groups were lying in wait. When we rolled into a new city, we were frequently greeted by these do-gooders. These are overwhelmingly young women. When their children have started school, there is a big hole in their lives, and agitating for a cause fills that hole. Usually they were waving signs, jumping up and down, and shouting about freedom and cruelty. Audi, our new bus driver, would lean out of his side window as he turned into the parking lot and yell, "Get a job, lady! Get a job!" Occasionally though, the protestors would chain themselves to the gates and temporarily stop us entering. Someone would have to get bolt cutters to release them.

When we arrived at the building, my first tasks were to find my teaching area, locate the school supplies, and get set up. Selecting my space in every building was the job of John, the performance director. It was wise to stay on his good side or I might end up in the boiler room. In fact, it could get much worse than the boiler room. I remember one building in Birmingham, Alabama, where my schoolroom was located alongside the early childcare area. The corridors were littered with cigarette butts, the floors unswept, the carpet unvacuumed. The schoolroom was an area behind curtains, next to the nursery. The rug rats and hip warts next door provided a Greek chorus to offset my performance. They howled in communal anguish. My voice could hardly be heard as they whimpered, shrieked, moaned, and sobbed for hours without ceasing. It was like some giant Eastern funeral with the mourners screaming, crying, and tearing their clothes to express grief. At other times, the TV drowned out both them and me. To make matters worse, whenever the noise abated, the moms pulled out the vacuums and started to clean. Another time, in the Armory in D.C. we ended up in a basement behind curtains. In the middle of class, a bat flew up out of a floor grate. The kids leaped to their feet and took off after it as it flapped around the place. Yeah, a boiler room isn't so bad!

The days followed each other in a blur of noise and color as we moved from city to city. As a novice, I never knew what to expect. After D.C., we had a good journey into Asheville, but what an arrival! When the locomotive was backing the flats into the train yard, the driver got carried away and backed it too far, right off the end of the tracks and onto the asphalt. It took out three vehicles, a silver truck, and two Blazers before it stopped. Still, the building reception was quite a plus. Television crews were waiting to film the acts for commercials. The catering service was soon doing double duty as all the circus people, schoolroom included, took advantage of the free goodies.

I soon got into the habit of coming to work early. Most days the elephants were still sleeping, dead to the world, huge bodies utterly relaxed, trunks lolling on the concrete floors. Later in the day they would be up, swaying from side to side, and poking clumps of hay into hairy mouths. First day in town I would have to find my school-books, which were initially stored in John's wardrobe trunk. What a job it was, getting them to the classroom! One schoolroom was along a balcony. We had to carry the school supplies upstairs on the first day, but the children helped carry them, and I had the advantage of being able to lock up at night. It's amazing how the children adapted to this loud and bustling atmosphere, busily doing their reading, writing, and drawing. Class just flew by.

That first year, there were fifteen children altogether. Five of them were young performers, but the rest were the children of performers and concessionaires. One of the youngest girls, Alessandra, introduced me to her parents, Janos and Nancy. They had met in California twelve years before and married in Budapest. Janos used to perform, but now he was working concessions (snow cones). This is a common progression in the circus. When you are too old to perform, concessions are an easy transition. Janos and Nancy had a mobile home, which was always parked close to the building. A home on wheels is so convenient for getting to and from work. Then, there is the additional advantage of possessing the vehicle that tows the home. It means that the family can get around in each city without waiting for the circus bus.

Another family that fitted into this world of performer-and-concessionaire was the Vargas family out of Mexico. Initially, five of my students were from the Vargas family of flyers or trapeze artists. Franco and Miguel were teenagers. Elvit, Ivan, and Alex were in the younger group. Later, I added Sebastian, another of the Vegas family children. He was only five years old, a plump little hippy with a long pony tail. It was obvious that he wanted to come to school too. He was cute, so I took him. That made six Vargases.

Then there was the Boger family. The two Boger brothers had an act involving buffalo, a long-horn steer, and ponies. There were four Boger children. The older two, Chris (fifteen) and Casey (thirteen), both performed in the act, which meant they got to bed late. They were in the later class. Little Katie and Whitney were in the younger school group. Since they did not perform, they could be in bed earlier and could be schooled first, before the show started.

In the first week, I slipped out between classes to get my picture taken and get a circus ID. Tina Gebel, the stepdaughter of Gunther, the famous animal trainer, strolled by. Clad in her gorgeous royal blue glitter gown, she made quite an impression.. Gunther, her stepfather, was now in charge of the animals of the Red Unit and had a big stake in the circus. This made Tina part of the circus aristocracy. Tina lived in the slipstream of Gunther's power and used it to great effect. She had married Eddie, an acrobat with a son, Lorenzo, by a previous marriage. Lorenzo, age six, was one of the younger group

I met several more of the mothers in the first weeks. Two of the Bulgarian acrobatic troupe had a teenage daughter, Gery, who performed with them. Another performing couple had a son, Nedielko. Then there were little Janos and Kazik whose parents were in concessions. Soon I saw Sergio, another of the concessionaires' kids, hanging out on the edge of the group. He looked about ten years old, but I learned that he had never been to class. I couldn't understand why. One day, after the last show, I caught the bus back to the train. I sat next to Nicole, one of the clowns. Nicole had given up an academic college scholarship to go to clown college and join the circus. She had been trying to help Sergio learn to read. It had been a hard struggle. Sergio told her that his brain may have been affected by the nuclear tests that had taken place in Nevada, near where he was born. I didn't think that there was any problem with Sergio's brain. Sergio's mother was French and his father was Mexican. Hearing nothing but French and Spanish spoken at home every day can't have helped his acquisition of English, and English is the language in which he was taught. I speak French and Spanish. I decided to work on his parents to enroll him in school. It's funny, but in this world, I didn't stand out for my language ability. I met people who were illiterate in ten languages.

It was quite a juggling act to fit in all the teaching sessions. The young five-to-eight-year-olds needed three hours in class, and the non-performing kids, four hours. The young performers slipped in at any time for at least three hours of work with a half-hour break. You might think that this shortchanged the circus kids in classroom hours, but school goes on all year. There is no such thing as summer vacation or spring break for circus kids. Travel steals part of our school hours, but Saturdays and Sundays are just normal workdays. At the end of each school day, unless we had school in an area that could be locked, the books had to be carried back to the wardrobe box. All the kids helped. Having parents working in plain view teaches the children what it takes to be an adult. They acquire a work ethic by example.

Circus life is amazing! It must have been something like this, living in a small English village a couple of hundred years ago. A local would know everybody in the village from all walks of life. He would know the farm laborers, the inn keeper, the blacksmith, the parson, and the lord of the manor. He would know whose bastard the village drab had borne, who was stealing chickens, and whether the lord's son preferred the shepherd, the shepherdess, or the sheep. The great thing about this village is that it moves along with us. We may not always remember what city we are in, but when we go into the local hangouts – into the malls, the restaurants, the bars – there are our fellow villagers. I remember standing at a street corner in one city. I asked a nearby pedestrian, "Excuse me. Where are we?"

"We're at North and Madison," came the reply.

"No, no, not that," I said. "What city are we in?"

When school was out, I had plenty of socializing to do. Back at the train I had met the most wonderfully fascinating people. The women of the train used to get together on a Thursday night. After a hard day's work we felt that we had a duty to unwind and refuel the engines for another day. We hauled out card tables and folding seats. With pot luck food and portable beverages we soon had a hen party going. The men of the train, the porters and engineers, envied us this outlet. They wanted in. Initially we were adamant. "No men! Only women are allowed." Still, there is no stopping a train crew guy when he wants to be included.

One evening, shortly after we women had settled into our folding chairs, a strange group of individuals appeared. It was the train crew. They had solved the gender problem. They had raided the housekeeping supplies and turned up in drag, festooned with hair pieces from rag mop heads and bodies clad in robes of flowered drapes and towels. How could we turn them away? Life was full and fun!

How well I slept now. The throb of the engine or the generator's shudder traveled along the couplings like a mother's heartbeat. The train was home.

CHAPTER 6

SCHOOL

It took a while before I knew everyone, and I was very impressed by the real circus people. Those who have been circus for generations have a different way of seeing things. Remember the lines from the old Shel Silverstein poem?

The gypsies are coming, the old people say,
To steal little children and take them away.

Well, according to circus people, the opposite is true. The parents would tell me, "Be careful! Don't let the townies get our children." The townies were the villains now, not the gypsies. The buildings where we played were new and strange to me. When one student needed to go to the bathroom, we all went. I couldn't take the risk that he might get lost, or worse.

Willie, the temporary teacher I replaced, had already told me about Lorenzo, a cute littl kid, with dark hair and big brown eyes. If only his personality lived up to his appearance! Lorenzo's mother, Cherry, had left him and her husband, Eddie, when Lorenzo was only two. Maybe going motherless for four years was to blame, but, no matter what the reason, Lorenzo was a wild child. Eventually Eddie married Tina Gebel, the stepdaughter of Gunther, the boss of the animal team. This gave Lorenzo powerful protectors. He could get away with behavior that would not be accepted in other families. Eddie, a dark-haired, talented acrobat, discounted Lorenzo's wildness. Eddie said that he, himself, never had any discipline till he joined the army. He thought that Lorenzo's behavior was normal and that we should just live with it. Of course, that meant that Tina and the teacher should just live with it.

Lorenzo, at age six, was already a standout when it came to vocabulary. The air rang with expletives when he felt angry or frustrated. The Vargas kids would try to contain him. "You shouldn't say the 'f' word, Lorenzo." "Lorenzo, you shouldn't say the 's' word." That didn't stop him though. He could curse like a seasoned sailor. Poor Tina! I sympathized with her problem but I didn't want to be the solution.

Lately Cherry, Lorenzo's mother, had shown some interest in him. She now lived and worked in Florida. She asked that Lorenzo come down to visit her for a while. Eddie and Tina were okay with that, so he flew down to join her. The visit went well. Lorenzo told us that his mother let him collect the tips in the bar where she was a waitress. Well, it seemed that he hadn't worn out his welcome and Cherry was up for another visit.

Tina was thrilled and grateful for the offer. She was desperately trying to arrange this. I welcomed the idea as much as Tina. A few weeks without Lorenzo would be good for me. He was slowly getting better. The grabbing and the language were not quite as bad. When he went ballistic, I had to physically restrain him and hold him tight on my knee. He would suddenly lose all that tension, as if he enjoyed the closeness. Poor little thing! He needed a mother. Tina was doing her best, but as a stepmother she was probably trying too hard. He needed some discipline mixed with the caring. He needed to be told "No," occasionally.

If that failed, I'd strangle him!

Still, Tina seemed to feel that school was organized purely for the benefit of her family, and that, if I were not taking care of Lorenzo, I had no value. She approached me with a suggestion.

"I'm Tina, Tina Gebel. My son, Lorenzo will be leaving for a month soon. He'll be flying out to spend some more time with his mother. If you plan to take a vacation, that would be a convenient time."

It would be convenient for her if I went away during this period and saved the circus some money! Obviously, the other kids didn't matter. Fortunately, Tina did not have the authority for this.

Years ago circuses used to perform under canvas. Great tents were erected wherever they performed, but nowadays this circus performs in the arenas of each city. No arena means no circus. These buildings are centered on the three-ring performance areas, surrounded by banked seating, multiple flights of stairs and huge curving corridors. These are lined on the outer side by assortments of offices, restaurants, dressing areas, and multipurpose spaces. The schoolroom can be in any of these.

I remember my first schoolroom with the circus, in the front restaurant bar of the arena. The small, nonperforming kids did not have to be up late, so they could have class early. My early students were six boys: Elvit, Lorenzo, Alex, Janos, Ivan, and Kazik, plus two girls: Alessandra and Katie. They were soon busily writing and drawing. It was amazing how the children just continued working no matter what the situation. They were excited by the new teaching aids though, particularly the spell-and-listen game, the new books, pencils, and erasers. Lunch was a potluck at the back of the ring: a welcoming feast of ethnic dishes served by a crowd of mothers of varying nationalities.

After lunch I had school for the performing children. There were four boys: Chris, Miguel, Franco, and Sergio, and two girls: Casey and Gery. These were generally older. When school ended we had a long haul to put away the schoolbooks in the performance director's wardrobe trunk. Still, the kids were great. They carried the books and equipment to the box without complaint.

Finally I was going to get my own box for the school supplies. Eric, the ringmaster may have precipitated this by getting upset at me for using his space. He shared a wardrobe trunk with John Dedo, the performance director, who allowed me to put my books in his half of the box. To pick up and return stuff to the trunk, a couple of times I had to enter rooms where Eric had been relaxing or dressing. I was also guilty of moving some of his mail across the table to put my books on the table edge. This, and the fact that I may have left the wardrobe trunk open, was evidently too much for his artistic temperament. An old circus superstition says that an open wardrobe trunk is bad luck. Still, I figured that if I got my own box, it would be good luck for me.

Sunday of my first teaching week was load-out time. We were ready to move on. I was exhausted and headachy. That morning I had the older kids mark our future path on a large map of the United States. Later they listened to the Shel Silverstein poem "The Acrobats." Miguel and Franco, members of the Vargas family of acrobats and concessionaires, loved this poem and its illustration. Gery Kehiava, from the Bulgarian troupe of acrobats, was inspired to write her own poem. Later, everyone did a journal entry about their favorite character. The little ones were lively, as usual, but better. We did a play – *Red Riding Hood* – then played a game, "What Time Is It Mr. Wolf?" I remembered this game from my childhood in England.

The kids loved the game. The Wolf stands with his back to the kids, who all stand behind a line some distance away. One of the pack asks the question, "What time is it Mr. Wolf?" The Wolf just makes up an answer. If the answer is eight o'clock, the kids have to advance eight paces toward the Wolf, three o'clock and they advance three paces. The questions continue as the kids get closer and closer and the steps get shorter and shorter. When the Wolf senses that the pack is very close and one kid asks the question again, instead of answering with a time of day, he suddenly shouts, "Dinner Time!" Then he spins around and chases the kids back toward the line. Whoever he catches is the next wolf. By the time we finished, everyone was exhausted. It was time to pack up, but they still had the energy to do a great job of packing away the equipment for me.

Circus children, on the whole, are warm, loving, and well-adjusted. These kids don't just have one or two doting parents; they have more than three hundred. I thought of all the people in that circus community as parents, since they knew the children and watched out for them. My classroom was often in full view on an area of a passageway. People would float by, lean over a working child and say, "Hey, that's really neat! Great work!" or "You've got to be kidding! You can do better than that! Pay attention! Listen to the teacher."

There were some very bright kids, but academically, as a group, they didn't usually measure up to young movie or theater actors who have stage mothers to push them. Circus kids go through a different nurturing program. When the parents are selected for their ability to walk into a cage full of lions, or swing across the roof of the center ring, they are being bred for guts – guts and talent. Even if they don't have these, they have a great work ethic and can always move on to concessions. Miguel was already part of the Vargas family act. He had the talent. He was great on the trapeze. It was obvious that he was destined to do the quadruple somersault in the future. Franco Vargas, on the other hand, had the wrong build. He was too husky to be a flyer. I gathered that new Vargas babies were examined soon after birth to see if they had the right physique to make trapeze material. If they didn't make that cut, there were always plenty of other positions.

The show must go on and these are the performers of the future. There were some exceptional students though. Chris Boger, whose family had the buffalo act, was a pretty bright kid. When he graduated from the Calvert Correspondence School, I enrolled him in the American Correspondence High School out of Chicago. Eventually he got his high-school graduation certificate and went on to a university. He planned to become a vet.

With parents to push for Chris, this opportunity came easily. The course cost quite a bit of money, but the circus paid. The Bogers were a valuable act. I had to push hard to get the same opportunity for Gery. When her parents returned to Bulgaria, she stayed on in the United States. Gery did prove herself valuable though, when the press came in for publicity. She knew how to be positive: how to field probing questions and paint circus life in glowing colors. Later, she showed her real talent. She rode a motorcycle in the Globe of Death. What an act! I remember it well. A group of performers on motorbikes rode around the globe at breakneck speed, sometimes parallel to the ground, sometimes totally upside down. It was terrifying. Only when the act ended, only when the bikers emerged and took their bows did the facts emerge. One by one, the bikers removed their helmets and took their bows. Only when Gery removed her helmet and shook loose her long dark hair, did the audience realize that a young girl had been a part of this terrifying act. What a response there was. The audience roared.

The circus moves on, but school is a constant. I enjoyed the travel, seeing the wooded hills of Pennsylvania yield to the flat cornfields of Ohio. We stopped in St. Louis for water. It was supposed to be a four-hour stop, but it was much shorter. I hoped that no one was left behind in Tulsa. What happened to it? Suddenly I was in Tucson, Arizona. Tulsa must have passed like a dream: quiet streets, a library and a courthouse right next to the arena. I do remember the courthouse though.

When the circus was setting up, I took the kids to see a trial. I had to pull Sergio out when he got the giggles, prompted by Ned's watch erupting into peals of bells and Miguel passing wind. Miguel was wearing a cast on his foot. He had tipped a water cooler on it.

Sergio was the funniest one to wear a cast. He was running along the back corridor of an arena and jumped up to touch a light fixture. As he jumped, he slipped and crashed down on his elbows. He broke both arms and had them set, elbows bent and crossed in front. Of course, there was the slight problem of going to the bathroom. Mother had to go with him and hold his you-know-what. Naturally, the kids got quite a charge out of that. They didn't overdo it though, because everybody loved Sergio.

After Tucson, it was time to head toward the west coast. There was so much to see, so much to experience. As we moved on from city to city, we absorbed the geography, the history, and the culture of this nation. I remember gazing in wonder at the stars on the sidewalk in Hollywood, honoring the greats of the entertainment business. There were frequent opportunities to enjoy what each location had to offer. In one city, Tim, our General Manager, arranged to swap circus tickets for entrance to the

I-Max movies. The older kids got to see *The Blue Planet* while the little ones saw *Beavers*. Eventually I figured out how to do this.

I loved this wheeler-dealer method of acquiring entrance to good field-trip locations. Washington D.C. is the best. One year I promised circus tickets to the guys in charge of the Tomb of the Unknowns if they let our kids place flowers on the tomb. First, the kids peeled off their circus logo T-shirts and turned them inside out. I had bought a couple of bunches of white roses on the street and got the kids to stand, holding the flowers, while taps was played. Afterwards they walked with the honor guard to place them. Before they went, Miguel was worried. "Are you sure it's okay, Mrs. R?" he said. "We're not American, we're Mexican,"

"Miguel," I told him. "You are showing respect. They will be honored."

Another great field trip was to the Statue of Liberty. We took the ferry to Liberty Island and then climbed the winding staircase to the top where we could see the amazing view from the crown. We took the elevator down. Here, at the base, reading Emma Lazarus's poem, "The New Colossus," I was in awe of the experience. My fellow chaperone, a gay guy from pyrotechnics, had a different take. "Well," he said. "I can honestly say that that is the first time in my life that I have been up a woman's skirt."

Finally we reached the west coast. Anaheim is a nice, clean, quality town with a building like a flying saucer. I was glad to leave though. My classroom was in the Bogers' dressing room, an area partitioned off by blue drapes suspended from cross poles. On one side was a card table with a rummy game constantly in progress. Beyond that, a Chinese gambling group periodically erupted into loud exchanges of abuse. The aroma of cooking fish floated over from the Mexican acrobats on the other side. Periodically we were treated to the blaring music of boom boxes. To add the final *coup de grâce*, the loudspeakers blasted us constantly with an ongoing account of the performance. There was no let-up with a six-pack (two three-show days) over the weekend. My head was spinning. God knows how we managed with the lessons, but we did. Funnily enough, the math survived the turmoil best. To do English, social studies, and so on requires some calm, but math can be done in a cyclone. With abstract numbers, we could blot out our surroundings.

The first time we were on this coast, we had Danny the giraffe with us. We had a special separate train wagon for the school, which was hauled off the flats and parked close to the train and close to the projects. Pete had just opened the door to take Danny out when he noticed a pack of local kids staggering off with two wardrobe trunks full of school books. He was too involved with Danny to stop them. He apologized for his inability to save our supplies. "Obviously they were desperate for an education," I observed. Pete laughed. "Yeah, that must be it."

CHAPTER 7

LOAD-IN AND SET-UP

It takes a lot of people to make a circus work, not just to perform, but to set up and organize each new building, drive the vehicles, take care of the animals, cook the food, and maintain the train. There is a rough division of labor between three crews: the train crew, the building crew, and the animal crew. At one time or another all of these guys can be found in the Pie Car, our train-coach version of an American diner with Formica topped tables and special of the day. The upscale people – the performers – don't eat there. Performers and administrators generally have cooking facilities in their rooms. They are from the right side of the tracks. Now, maybe I was in that category, but I liked to eat in the Pie Car. I liked the regular guys, and where else could I get all the gossip?

The workmen file in past the food counter, order, pick up, and pay for their meals before sitting down. These are a mixture of long-term workers and recent hires. Long term in the circus might mean just two years at the job. Change is constant though. Workers come and go, so the circus has to be careful. Men who are penniless or off the street cannot be given real money up front or they might just disappear without doing any work. Still, they have to eat, so they are given dukies to hold them over. Dukies are paper script that is handed out to the new men if they are penniless. These are worth money only in the Pie Car and Pie Car Junior. They are deducted from pay later.

The dukies keep the men honest. They also have to sleep in the bunk car with the rest of the new hires. This can be rough on them. The problem is not the train or the job. It is the unknown qualities of the men they work with. Sometimes these get violent; sometimes they steal. In time a man can earn better accommodation and better money, but first he must pay his dues: he must survive the bunk-car.

I was always interested in what drove these men to join the circus. Some of them were adventurers, thirsting for a new experience. Some were running away from bad situations or responsibilities.

Dave from building crew had left a bad situation. He had been working and earning his keep since he was thirteen. At age fifteen his father kicked him out. Dave just packed up his belongings and headed out with half the contents of the house. When his father protested, Dave produced the receipts. He had paid for the stuff.

James, a cook in the Pie Car belonged to the last group. He just heard that, back in New York City, his son had been disciplined at school for some misdeed. James walked out on his girlfriend and son years ago, but he still felt that nobody had the right to discipline the boy except himself. He had the choice between staying and being a father, or joining the circus and avoiding child support payments. The circus won!

Then, of course, there was the possibility that we might have someone from the ten most-wanted list in the bunk car. I mentioned this in the Pie Car one day. "Hey, I'm not on the ten most-wanted list," offered one of the guys. "I joined because nobody wanted me." Sometimes a joke covers up a lot of pain.

What a day! We pulled into town at 9:30 a.m. after a 4:30 a.m. start-and-stop process. At midday we were still waiting for the equipment to be unloaded. The train had been broken into two sections. Through my window I could see the carriages on a huge flatbed being coupled together. A tractor up front adjusted its train of wagons forward and back in response to whistles, while a couple of men waited to hitch up the next trailer as soon as the couplings were in line.

The day was devoted to unloading the train and setting things up at the building. There was no show, so those of us who were not needed for set-up busied ourselves with chores. That day, I went on the laundry and supermarket trip. Audi was now driving the bus on a regular basis. Our last driver had been moved to another job. He had lost his license for forty-five days. His old New York tickets had come back to haunt him. Audi was quite an improvement. It was amazing how he could maneuver the bus through spaces with less than an inch of clearance, without even scraping a side or losing a mirror. He was great at dropping everyone off, right at the door of their coach. Gus, a new guy but an old circus hand, came along with us.

Gus was a character: a long, lean, sun-toasted cowboy. He was a charmer and a font of anecdotes. The true ones were undated, but if the story was preceded by, "I remember in July of 84", then it was probably lies – entertaining lies however. One undated story was about Tim Holan. The men were in Tim's truck, waiting to cross a railway line. A procession of flatbeds was juddering backwards and forwards over the crossing, while the circus vehicles waited for an opportunity to pass. Eventually Tim lost patience. After one backward surge of the train, and before it could start forward again, Tim jumped out of the truck and pulled the trip lever connecting two sections of the train. The engine took off without half the flats. The circus vehicles rode across the empty tracks and off to work. Rick said that a computer reading of weight would have soon let the engine driver know what had happened.

The following morning, the circus bus was ready to take us all to the building. That day, a new African American worker ran to catch us. Mark Gebel held the bus for him. I was glad that the new worker didn't sit next to the man on the seat opposite me. The third tattoo on this guy's arm was the White Power sign, complete with swastika. Later on I saw a beauty: a skull with a green beret and a sword behind it. I wonder what that signified?

When I got off the bus, I saw Mad Max and Chalk Eye for the first time. These were chestnut horses that had arrived recently. The new stable hands who were responsible for them were terrified. Of course, the old guard had laid on a story. They love to jerk the chains of the new hires. According to the tall-tale brigade, Chalk Eye should be called Dead Eye. He had supposedly killed one man already and had been on a three-month training course to redirect his urges. Mad Max? Well, the name said it all. Time would tell how many of the new animal crew lasted. Last year, we lost fifteen in California. The animals themselves played a big part in deciding who stayed on. If the elephants took a dislike to someone , they got the message across fast. When an elephant wants to intimidate someone it will make itself look bigger. If the ears are outstretched, then look out! The horses are exactly the opposite. Ears up means good temper, but if the ears are flat back, watch out!

In the building, I bumped into Pete, the stable boss, chortling about the results of his Mad Max stories. These stories were evolving by the minute. Max was now being described as the racehorse that savaged his jockey and was sentenced to twelve years hard labor in the circus. Mad Max lived up to some of the fiction. He kicked Lisa and two of the men the first time he was led up the ramp onto the train. Lisa, who had the barnyard animal act, had spent a few days walking Max along a detached ramp in the building. The hope was that when he got back on the train, he'd be okay. The men still thought of him as the killer horse though. His rep was growing.

The animals always kept things exciting. At the start of the afternoon show, the crew arrived at the ring, minus one llama. It had taken off and was running around the parking lot. The call of "Llama loose!" came over the radio and sent men scattering in all directions. The poor llama finally gave himself up and was in much better shape than the men. The guys, exhausted, found relief in banter. An African American guy was told, "Hey, man, you're a minority."

"What do you mean, man?"

"I hate to be the one to tell you, man, but you're black."

"No, I'm not. I'm teasing baby brown."

"My God, you're getting like Sid. He says he's pecan brown."

Later that day, I rode home with Mark, James, Deana, and forty gallons of milk, destined for the Pie Car. The Shetland ponies were being walked back to the train by a couple of black guys singing "Old MacDonald Had a Farm." For some reason James took offense and jumped out of the van to confront them. "You got a prob.?" he challenged them. They walked on. Sensible guys! On the way back we picked up the beers, $9 for twenty-four. During the train ride to the next venue James charged $1.50 a can.

There are always people who can make money in the circus world. The Polish guys, Louis and Company from the animal crew had come over from Europe with Gunther. They take care of the horses and also have a gambling and money-lending business going. It was wise to stay out of their games. In the evenings and on the long train journeys they played interminable card games for money. The crew gets paid on Saturdays. By Wednesday many were broke, and till the next pay day, they had to beg, borrow, or steal to eat, or sometimes just do without. When they borrowed, they ended up paying exorbitant interest. Tempers flared.

On Tuesday, I got a lift back in the truck with Dave and Gerry. Dave took me to the grocery store and then drove me right to my coach. How gentlemanly these men can be when treated with a modicum of civility. They don't always get it. Dave was looking forward to going out to dinner with Teresa. He's happy to have Teresa as a friend and occasional dinner date. He'd just been brushed off pretty brutally by another show-girl who told him plainly to his face,

"You're fat! I can't be seen with someone like you. It would hurt my image." What a world!

Connected to the rest of the train, it's harder to give up the vices. The men bought quantities of alcohol and cigarettes, some for themselves, and some to sell at inflated prices.

The usual banter was going on. Drago and Alison were going bowling.

"I like bowling, but I'm no good at it," confessed Drago.

"That's okay," someone countered. "You can still enjoy something, even if you are no good at it. Like sex!"

Rick was in a fight and had his hand injured for taking his roommate Chris's beer and selling it. Rick came roaring back with an elephant hook and got slugged by Gerry. What a disaster! These men can't handle free time without getting into trouble.

CHAPTER 8

LOAD-OUT

A travel day! After the last Sunday show it was time to move on. As the acts closed in the final performance, the building crew and train crew were busy towing the animals, wagons, and equipment to the train. The men hustled, driving tractors and pulling wagons and equipment back from the building. The final show had ended at 7:30 p.m., but since we had to be out of the building by 11:00 p.m., everything possible, the circus bus included, had been preloaded on the flats. A rented bus ferried most of us back to the train. We passed the horses, llamas, and camels trotting along the road flanked by their usual audience of locals.

Sometimes the stock cars could be parked on a railroad spur close to the arena. This saved the animals a long walk back through the streets to the train. We couldn't do this in New York City though, so a procession of twenty-one elephants had to be walked through the midtown tunnel to the train in Queens. Since this involved closing the tunnel to traffic, it was done at three in the morning. The poor elephants must have been as exhausted as the crew who sleepwalked with them. In most locations a small audience of locals turned up to watch them get aboard. The elephants were loaded into the first two stock cars at the front of the train.

The elephants always go up front because the engine has to cushion the momentum of the stock cars if it has to brake suddenly. Those elephants literally weigh tons and when braking, their weight is thrown against the engine. Obviously the brakes have to be in very good shape. If they were further back, their weight could jackknife the train. The horses and zebras were in the next car after the elephants.

The coaches where the performers, crew, and concessionaires lived came after the animal cars. At the end of the train were the flats: long metal platforms onto which the wagons and circus vehicles would be rolled and secured. The cats were always kept in their holding wagons on the flats when we traveled.

The bus did several runs to deliver the workers back to the train. Some of our aristocracy, the upper-level acts and administrators, drove their cars back, so these could be loaded onto the flats before they retired to the comfort of their coaches. Those people with cars who didn't rate a place on the flats either drove them on to the next location, or paid someone else to deliver their vehicles.

Finally, when all the work was finished, the heavy metal step stools were moved up onto the vestibules and the doors were secured. Once the workers were safe on board, the last vehicle to roll onto the flats was the circus bus. In the next city it would be the first off, ready to take the riggers and later, the concession workers, to the building. The riggers were men with heads for heights. They had to climb up into the scaffolding at the top of the arena and attach the anchors and cables for the equipment. At the end of a long day, it was finally time for bed. I was lucky. The crews would be laboring far into the night.

The following morning, I awoke at 4:00 a.m. We still hadn't moved but the train crew guys were loading the flats alongside my compartment. I went out onto the vestibule to watch them sliding a wagon next to a truck and securing them both with chains from their brace points to the sides of the flats, with the chain boxes fitting into a track at the edge. Once the vehicles were secured, we moved quickly. The journey was short, but eventful. At 7:00 a.m., while only fifty miles out of town we hit a truck, a semi. The truck had been stopped. The driver had seen our lights and was watching the train approach. He rolled forward onto the track and was hit broadside. I heard that the driver and truck were tossed forty feet. The wreck had to be cut in half to load it onto a tow truck. The driver was alive, but due for a long hospital stay.

We pulled into town at 9:30 a.m. after a 4:30 a.m. start-and-stop progress. The train was split into two or three sections, which were parked on parallel tracks. At twelve noon we were still waiting for equipment to be unloaded. Opposite me, the train crew was moving the vehicles onto a huge flatbed. A tractor up front adjusted its train of carriages forward and back in response to whistle commands. Men waited to hitch up the next trailer when the coupling was in line. Dave, the big guy with long, dark, curly hair was in charge again.

In New Haven, our riggers had traveled ahead to get ready for us. They had been in the building since 2:00 a.m., anchoring supports for trusses into the top girders. The black fly beams, studded with canister lights, lay upon the ground, wheels collapsed under them. These had to be rolled back and forth to get them into the building, then raised up under the trusses, with a profusion of cables to connect them to lights and sound. A team of men struggled to assemble the globe of death, the enormous crisscrossed ball of steel in which the motor bikes roar around. The globe is assembled on site from massive, heavy sections. While assembling half of the bottom hemisphere, with five men pushing and bracing, the assembly tipped, falling on top of Frank. It hit his upper arm, bending him over and pinning him to the ground.

He was yelling with pain as the crew lifted the assembly off him. Soon, the paramedics arrived. I could see his feet twitching. I thought it was the electrical discharge from a broken spine. He was sedated, placed on a board, braced into place and carried off on the stretcher bed. Later that afternoon he was back to kick the globe. His arm was in a sling. He'd had stitches, but fortunately, no bones were broken. The doctor had urged him to sue. The trouble was that there was no one in charge of the set up and they hadn't put the bracing bar in place first. The man who used to be in charge of setting up the globe had just been promoted to ring overseer and no replacement had been named. Suing the circus would not be easy. We move on quickly from state to state, so legal jurisdiction would be hard to establish. Then, these men are too used to being kicked around. They don't want to take on The Man. After the morning's accident I walked too close to the globe. The guys were quick to let me know the danger. "Hey, Teach, move away from there," one of them yelled. "You don't wanna be a waffle, do you?" A waffle? I looked at the crisscrossed sections of steel and knew just what he meant.

When the riggers have been delivered to the building, it is the turn of concessions. Many of the concession stand owners had their own transportation and parked their trailers close to the building. The lower-level concessionaires had Spartan accommodation on the train, for which they paid a nominal rent. They arrived at the arena early and sat in the banked seats waiting for Mike, the concession manager. Mike had already allocated areas for the various stands, cotton candy, snow cones, souvenirs, etc. Once everyone was seated, he gave instructions specific to the building and administered a speech of motivation. He let them know what a useless, lazy, good-for-nothing bunch they were. I usually sat among them and took the dressing down. I figured it was good for my soul.

If we arrived too late to have a show on arrival day, I would leave the building and shuffle off to the mall for retail therapy. Finding my way back to the train could be a problem. Frequently we were parked in bad districts and, even with a taxi, the final leg, alongside and over railroad tracks at night, was scary. A good solution was to find a local bar close to the train. There I could be sure to find some of the crew. Usually they would walk me home, and if the vestibules were too high, they would be happy to push me up with a hand to the ass. They are so helpful!

I saw Dave again, in charge of a team of men unloading at the building. There was a jumble of guys with walkie-talkies, and tractors galore to pull out the garish floats and the animal cages filled with various pieces of equipment. Finally the big white trailers arrived, each with four square windows framing the occasional face of a tiger. The organized chaos is impressive: Mark, Kelly, Menudo, and many others on tractors came charging through the ramp opening down to the level where the animals are housed. The tractors – Fords, Kubotas, and others – were loaded with winches, forklifts, boots, and carrying chocks, which could be swiftly released and fitted to the underside of the tracks.

The ride into town had been an eye opener. As Gus was driving a tractor trailer and pulling a line of cat cages into town, Tim got through to him on the radio. "Just look to your right as you pass the next cross-road," he ordered. Gus followed directions. There was a topless bar! The girls had all turned out wearing only their bloomers to watch the cars pass. "It took me a half hour to clear that crossing," said Gus.

Leaving the stadium later that night, I saw a car parked under the bridge by the tracks – a dark Honda Prelude with a plate reading ECSTASY. A platinum blond was sitting in it, counting a wad of bills. I wonder what her livelihood is?

CHAPTER 9

THE GRAND CIRCLE TOUR

When Ringling puts together a new show, the train is set up to house all the necessary people, animals and equipment. The Unit will tour for two years, traveling from city to city on a roughly preordained path. The first year is what I call the grand circle tour. Starting in January from winter quarters in Tampa, it stops in a few Florida cities before heading up to Birmingham, Alabama. The length of stay in each city depends on the projected size of the audience. This may be as short as two days. Then there are several stops in North Carolina, Virginia, and New Jersey. By March the circus arrives in New York City where I interviewed. Here, the circus may stay for up to two months.

After New York the tour progresses through the New England states. That was where I joined the circus. Now, after a few years, the path ahead is predictable. After cruising up the northeast coast we head inland, through Pennsylvania, then we turn southwest and start to move in a roughly counterclockwise path around the United States. First the train heads down to Tulsa, on to Arizona, then west to southern California. Finally, it's up the west coast to Oregon, across the coastal range to Salt Lake City, then over the Rockies to Denver. I used to live in Denver and still have friends there. It was great getting together and visiting Larimer Square again. The stay was too short though, and soon it was on to Chicago, before moving south again to winter quarters in Florida.

The routine in each city is always the same. As the acts close in the final performance, the building crew and train crew do load-out, towing animals and equipment to the stock cars on the train. The first animals out of the building are the elephants, shuffling along with trunks clutching the tails of the elephants ahead, the men with bull hooks jogging to keep abreast. The horses come next, trotting in pairs, and finally, camels, llamas, and other animals. The big cats always travel in large wagons that are loaded onto the flats at the back of the train. Huge feline faces can be seen, pressed against the high, square windows.

Later, after the show has finished, the circus bus and other vehicles deliver the train dwellers to the coaches, where most of us lived. Accommodations varied according to status. Gunther, the unit boss, and his family occupied one-and-a-half coaches; a ringmaster, a general manager or a top act might get a quarter to a half of a coach. Regular performers, personnel, and crew had single or double rooms. The young clowns slept in tiny rooms or bunkettes in their own coach. Dancers had small rooms in a similar set up. The lower level concessionaires paid rent for narrow bunks crammed into small single rooms while the new hires lived in the bunk car.

Not everyone traveled on the circus train. A lot of people, permanent concessionaires and performers with their own animals or equipment moved in private vehicles. Performers with special acts always had to transport their animals and equipment themselves. The circus didn't want to be responsible for carrying a troupe of baboons, chimpanzees, or other exotic creatures. Animals can die in transport and law suits cost money.

I remember one particular load-out, when we were about to move out of New England. The schedule was tight. Instead of traveling home to the train the usual way, we had a private bus that night. It being a Sunday, the final show ended at 7:30 but since we had to be out of town by 11:00 p.m., everything possible, the circus bus included, had been preloaded on the flats. We passed the procession of animals trotting along the road. It was going to be a long train journey to the next city. It would seem longer. Before I boarded the train, I smoked my last cigarette and tossed the rest into the trash.

The trip to Tulsa took more than two days, leaving after the show late Sunday and arriving Wednesday morning. My coach wasn't connected to the rest of the train during travel, so there was no way I could beg, borrow, or steal a cigarette. The doors of the adjoining coaches were locked. The only time I could visit other coaches was when we were stationary, and I could climb in and out of vestibules. For nearly three days I went cold turkey. There were no other smokers in my coach – nobody to borrow from. By the time we reached Tulsa, I was cured, no longer a nicotine addict, smoke-free at last! Of course, my screams of anguish may have disturbed some of the other occupants of my coach, but it was for a good cause. Most smokers don't have the opportunity to go cold turkey like this, but it's a great way to give up the habit. A regular person would have to arrange to be incarcerated for a few days - maybe commit a minor crime. In jail, though, you are probably allowed to smoke.

Well, now that the smoking habit was beaten, it was time to work on the body. I needed to exercise, but calisthenics were impossible in a room the size of a postage stamp. At that time I lived in a 7-by-7½-foot room. I had come down in the world. Allocation of accommodation follows a preset formula, according to your role in the show. Unfortunately the teacher is a wild card. Sometimes, if the current general manager had happy memories of his school days, I got better accommodations, but bad memories meant disaster for me. I had lived in a double room when I first joined the circus, but my accommodations changed according to the whims of the general manager, and general managers changed frequently. The desk seat in 14 wagon, where our current manager sat, was commonly known as an ejection seat, or sometimes a rejection seat.

Anyway, a new manager meant a new deal. Everything depended upon his interpretation of my worth. At one time I had my own bathroom, a futon couch with a separate bunk, a full-sized refrigerator, and a stove. I was in the big time! I could entertain. I could stir up a good curry and make steam come out of my guests' ears. Unfortunately, the good times didn't last long. One unit manager must have had really bad memories of his Catholic school education, which I exacerbated by dressing up as a nun for Halloween. He put me in a tiny basic single with a bunk, a sink and a miniature fridge. The room was so small that I protested.

"My contract says that I should be accommodated as staff," I wailed. "Instead, I'm in a room smaller than a cell on death row in Florida."

"Staff," he retorted, withering me with a glance, "is who I say is staff."

That put me in my place! Anyway, I still had to do something about exercise. Locked in that tiny little room, my body was turning to jello. In the next city, in the mall, I bought an exercise tape: Angela Lansbury's "Positive Moves, a Personal Plan for Fitness and Well-Being at Any Age." I would lie on my bunk in that narrow room pointing my remote up at the TV in the corner of the room. Boy, was that woman good! She bounced, she jumped, she twisted and stretched. She sure did work hard! I lay back and watched her go through the whole routine. If I felt really mean, I made her do it twice.

The circus train obviously provided a bit of color in the small towns. Groups of people came out to wave as we passed through. In time I had become friends with Eric, our gay ringmaster. One day, he asked me how I enjoyed being with the circus. Since I came from England originally, I couldn't resist informing him that when we passed through the little towns, I stood out on the vestibule and waved like the Queen. I demonstrated the arm movement – all from the elbow, with wrist and hand immobile. He grinned and responded. "I wave like a queen too," he said.

The train is quite a place. It has to provide everything that the circus workers need for day-to-day living. One car contains a huge generator that provides power for the whole train. That takes a lot of fuel. We need AC in the summer and heating in the winter. Apart from the engines, we had to be completely self-sufficient. The engines were something else though. I had always thought of them as being a part of the train, but they are not! The train is the line of stock cars, coaches, and flats that are pulled by the engine or locomotive. The train belongs to Ringling, but the engines belong to the companies that own the rails, companies that must be paid big-time for the service they provide.

Lengths of track from a couple of miles to several hundred miles can be owned by individual companies like South Pacific, CSX, or Santa Fe Railroad. Whenever the train comes to the end of one company's track, it may be necessary to stop and change to the next company's engines. Now, the train is more than a mile long. On relatively flat runs, it can be pulled by one engine, leased from the track owner. If the terrain is rugged, it takes more than one engine to pull us. Going over the Rockies can involve as many as four engines at a time. On a long trip we had to stop periodically to fill up with water or to change engine crew. The trainmaster had to be constantly on call to keep in touch with the engine and train crew and plan for the needs of the train as we moved along. Moving this train from venue to venue must cost a fortune. When the economy takes a downturn, the arenas are half empty. How do we break even? One trainmaster told me that he suspected we were laundering Mob money.

After Tulsa, we headed southeast to Tucson, and then on to Phoenix. We were now in desert country, and the hot sun beat down on us mercilessly. Aluminum foil had been fixed to the corridor windows to reflect the light and give us some protection from the glare, but nothing seemed to counteract the sun's intensity. The heat of summer was too intense and when the time came to leave, we were all ready.

The train from Phoenix to San Diego pulled out at 5:45 a.m. We passed through vast stretches of desert, then a lake, and at the far side, an immense dump of powdered and crushed chemical concentrate. The landscape seemed unreal – tampered with. From the track, the land stretched out flat for a half mile or more; later a long, low range of yellow sand dunes obscured the distance. This low rolling swath of sand had a man-made feel as if it had been put there by bulldozers to obscure – what? I was getting paranoid. Nearly 3:00 p.m. and we passed through a long valley with more windmills that I ever thought to see in my life – thousands of them: thick, round posts supporting long white stalks, each topped by three black propellers. Suddenly the rain poured down. A treat for the desert! Soon we passed rigs and pumps, machines scraping and sucking at the earth.

After San Diego, we travel north up the coast. Our northernmost destination was Portland, Oregon. The journey there was slow. We were blocked by a derailment and had to bypass it by switching onto the Santa Fe tracks. The Southern Pacific line on which we were traveling had to send for a Santa Fe pilot to take us onto their tracks and back onto the Southern Pacific line. Delays were a drag, but sometimes, a dramatic drag, and I liked to know what was happening.

Eventually, we left Portland and were en route to Salt Lake City, rocking along as we climbed through the deciduous forests into the pines. The land is beautiful – unspoiled lakes and mountain ridges as far as the eye can see. From the vestibule I stared out at the rocky out-crops, the pine-coned treetops rising into view from the valley below. The air was cool and fresh. The aluminum foil had been peeled off the corridor windows. Summer was coming to an end and we were heading into cooler regions. The AC was still blasting full strength. A full moon rose on the left. From the right vestibule door I could see a herd of deer grazing.

After Salt Lake City, with the help of several engines, we moved over the Rockies and on toward Denver. We had reached the final leg of the journey. Next came Minneapolis, St. Paul, and Milwaukee. Wyoming introduced us to dry, windswept, high country. Snow banks and barbed wire fences lined the tracks. A small deer had attempted, without suc-cess, to leap the fence. Its dried carcass hung across the top wire, hinged from the hip pivot. What a death!

The year was coming to an end. Heading toward Milwaukee, the lakes were beautiful, their banks strewn with leaves from the bare trees, the boats pulled up on the banks, ready for winter. Beside them stood piles of cordwood. The smell of yeast was overpowering. At least, the wind was from the breweries and not the slaughter yard. Finally, we arrived.

Thank God it was laundry day. Audi had scoped out the area, so that there was a convenient supermarket for me and a bar for the guys, mercifully close to the train. Gary and Jo, from the Pie Car, pounded on the Laundromat window on their way to the bar. They gave me a sip of their carrying fluid: bourbon. They told me that Bobby Miller, the train engineer, hadn't done his laundry for weeks now. Even his favorite pet lizard, which usually sleeps gripping his arm, had moved up into the top bunk.

The next stops would be Rosemont and Chicago. Chicago is no picnic in the winter. I lived here in my first year in the United States, and learned what "below zero" meant. When the time came to head south to winter quarters in Florida, we would all be ready. We could enjoy the passage home to friends and family. Finally, the nature of the land had changed. The earth became richer. We could see grain silos, oil derricks, and propane tanks. Cattle grazed in the harvested lands. Stretches of bare earth waited for winter to work the soil.

What an experience it is to see this country through the windows of a train. It is truly America the Beautiful.

CHAPTER 10

ON THE RAILS

In the first year of a circus tour, the unit does the grand circle of the United States. In the second year they never even cross over the Rockies. They sometimes go over the border into Canada, and one year we even went into Mexico. Still, they cover a lot of track, so everything has to be in top shape. You never know when there will be problems.

I bought a scanner from Radio Shack in the last city. One of the guys gave me the wavelength for the train chatter. I listened in while our trainmaster tried the old "thirsty elephant" story on the train track people. "Hey, Switchman, our elephants are thirsty and desperate for water. If you don't get us to a water stop fast, they might rock the train off the tracks."

That wouldn't work anyway, because it was a faulty axle that slowed us. It had been giving problem readings on the tracking equipment for a while now. Lord knows what the cause was – some equipment dragging perhaps. There was no hot box – whatever that meant! Our crew and the Southern Pacific crew checked it. If it gave an unfavorable reading, the last flats would have had to be cut out of the train and left to be adjusted and picked up later. Since they probably carried vehicles essential to the performance, this could have been catastrophic.

I lay on my bunk for hours, clutching the scanner. Bits of chatter on the train journey held my attention. Two men were hiding in 54 coach.

There was a 9:40 emergency stop. A hose had popped. At 10:20 we had a second emergency stop. Fire under coach 57! "What's that? That's my coach!" I leaped up, paused only to refresh my lipstick, and headed for the door when I heard, "Correction. That's coach 37." We were finally turning east and crossing back over the Coastal Range.

It was great entertainment, keeping in touch with what was going on during transit. For instance, during the last trip, there were problems. There were trespassers in one of the coaches. Then, one of the flats had brake problems and needed to be cut out and worked on during the water stop. We lost power temporarily on 31 pump. Finally, the zebras got in with the ponies again. We needed some latches in the stock cars so that they wouldn't open so easily. Eventually though, all was ready.

"Trainmaster, here we go," said the engine driver.

"Okay, let's boogie," came the reply from Taddy, our new trainmaster.

Now a message from Bobby, farther down the train. "Taddy, I've a woman on the train who doesn't work here. She needs to get off."

"Which car?"

"Number 47."

"Okay, I'll get back to you. Next signal stop and she's off."

"Hey, the canvas strap on a wheel wagon is broken."

"Jo, try to rig it with rope until the next stop. That's ETA 5:30."

"A heat indicator is showing problems on axle 228."

"What do you mean? There's no axle with that number!"

"Hey, the South Pacific people are going to check the whole train. The guys from 42 are going to check the flats."

"The problem is probably in car 44/45. We're looking for a hot box."

The journey here was slow. There was a succession of crises with the usual radio chatter. We were going to be late again.

We went by the remains of a train wreck: a derailment. There were twelve cars and an engine with a crew of men taking it apart to haul away as scrap. It can't have happened very long ago. Dave, the maintenance train engineer, told us later that the engine driver had been thrown clear. Although he was pretty banged up, he had run two miles back along the track to a call box where he was able to stop the Amtrak train only three miles behind them. That was a close call!

We were now in the land of the High Plains Drifter. This land was flat with distant mountain ridges. The sand flats were dotted with tufts and bumps of grey-green desert plants. Shiny mineral deposits glittered in the sand on the surface of vast shallow lagoons. There were few signs of life. A couple of gulls floated in the lake beyond my window. The train had stopped for water and I clambered down onto the powdery white alkali flats, my feet sinking in the sand. There were no rattlesnakes in evidence. I moistened my finger, bent down and tasted the white crust – salt! A double track led us through a lake. Trains hurtled past the vestibule – bi-levels carrying coal for the power plants.

With the Coastal Range behind us we played Salt Lake City and then continued east, over the Rockies to Denver and beyond. Trainmaster to the Engine Driver, "Hey, I'm spotting for water. I need the keys to the possum belly to get horse blankets. The windows are open on 32. Two of the horses are shaking with cold. Every time we stop I've got to fight with you drivers about the speed limit. You wanna do thirty-five to forty. I say I'm gonna unload one of the horses. I'll beat you there." I understood his frustration. We were two hours behind and we would need all our time to set up in Minneapolis.

Finally, time was on our side. The engine driver had speeded up. We were two hours ahead of time now and almost at our destination, only four hours from Minneapolis. I was hoping that we'd be there in time to do something with the evening, but no, it was not to be. The next stretch of track was so tilted that we had to crawl into town. I was rolling off the bed. The Pie Car couldn't fry an egg without it sliding off the grill. Still, we were on the final leg of the journey. Soon we would play Chicago and then start the long journey home.

CHAPTER 11

THE COLD

Pulling into Rosemont, Illinois, in November it was thirty-four degrees. It felt like two degrees with the wind chill factor. Frozen pools lined the tracks. My sink was stopped up – probably ice. I cured it with salt. I remembered from my days as a chemistry teacher that salt water freezes at a lower temperature than pure water. Rosemont was having a record cold snap. The generators were working overtime to keep up with the demands. They consumed fuel like crazy and the system couldn't keep up. As the power kept shutting off, we scrambled for lighters and candles.

One morning I had to get into the building early for a publicity interview, so I went to check the bus times. Gary was alone in the Pie Car. A sign promoted a breakfast of scrambled eggs and cheese, but his next disgruntled customer pushed the plate back at him. "No cheese," he complained. Gary reached across and tossed a slice of cold cheese on top of the eggs. "But it's cold!" the man complained.

Gary handed him a long-blade kitchen knife, handle first, then turned his back. "You wanna go at me?" he asked. "Feel free. Everyone else has."

"No problem, man," said his customer, shuffling away with his scrambled egg and cold cheese.

Chicago can be a miserable city for the circus, particularly in winter. The train is parked downtown. The projects are on one side, but on the other side is a police training zone for fast car chases. This makes a great side show. The building is in a bad area too. To walk one block to the sandwich shop, Mike, a backstage hand escorted me. Elvis from the animal crew swore he'd been mugged earlier. He certainly had a great shiner, but Pete, the stable boss had probably given that to him. Pete had the sore hand to prove it.

We were so confined by the danger of the location that people were getting edgy. Roland from 45 car went to the hospital in a flashing ambulance. Someone in 45 had been stoned out of his mind, and had been standing in the corridor with the door open. Mikey's father asked him to close the door because it was cold. The man refused and Roland came out of his room to add his weight to the request. "Close the damn door," he said. For his trouble, he got hit over the head with a baseball bat. Taddy told the police that it hadn't happened on the train. He didn't want them involved. The drug trade is big money and the sellers can get violent if someone makes trouble for them. Roland swore that he didn't know who had hit him. The attacker was thrown off the train, but no one goes after the pushers who feed the violence.

The train yard was hellish. The dirt track through the yard to the main road was a mile or more of potholes and gullies, filled up with water and mud. Leshik's wife (a ball buster, according to the men) came striding into the Pie Car with a "What the hell are you-all doing, just sitting around in here?" The guys cringed and placated. Later they made plans to throw sticks into the mud puddle for her dog.

Menudo arrived late to drive the animal crew to the building. His excuse was, "I got caught in a funeral." Chris gave him a hard time. "It will be your funeral next time," added Menudo.

Next morning in the Pie Car I found the three Daves discussing the freeze problems. Lines were frozen all over the train so that many people couldn't get water. Dave, the Head Porter (we all called him Mr. T.

because he was married to T (short for Theresa)) had a few suggestions, but they were not well received.

"No way, Dave," replied Dave Walker and Dave H.

"Sure it will work," countered Mr. T.

"Shut up," said Dave Walker. "You don't know what you're talking about."

"That's never stopped me before!"

Thank God we were moving on. We figured that nothing could be worse than a Chicago winter, but we were wrong. The cold followed us. In the next city, power died during the intense freeze. The heating tapes that prevent the pipes from freezing went off and we lost water all over the train. Pumps, tanks and pipes froze and cracked. I finally got water back on Friday after seven days without. I had managed to get three gallons up front and was given another gallon later but that was nowhere near enough. Washing hair in a half cup of water and shampoo was an experience. Soon I learned to shower at the building in the women's bathroom. Stripping naked at my age and using one of those larger communal tiled relics reminiscent of Auschwitz is not my bag, especially when one is joined by lithe young dancers with *Playboy* bodies – it's demoralizing!

The weather dominated our world now. Snow and freezing rain on Wednesday crippled our transportation. All the pumps froze, so our water supply was nonexistent. Originally, when the circus train had been put together, the plan had been to install the pipes within the coaches but they were put underneath to preserve space. Still, if the generators hadn't failed, the heat strips would have protected the lines, but the severe cold put too much strain on the generators. We were lucky to have any heat at all. Water was now a luxury and we'd been without for too long. I pitied the people with cars and trailers. Alan and Mori's mothers had no heat in their camper and huddled together for warmth. Those with money moved into hotels, but still had the problems of cracked radiators, engine blocks, and dead batteries.

We had plumbers crawling around under the train. We were at the edge of a spread of the tracks and our adjacent track was busy. As a train swept by the Pie Car, a wit asked, "Any plumbers in the cow catcher?" The train crew had the miserable job of loading the flats and putting the train together – cold work. Pukie Eddie was wearing Bear boots today. He came in for some teasing about his electric socks shorting out in the puddles. "Maybe we can get an extension cord and run you from the train," was one suggestion.

There were problems with the Pie Car Junior today. What a day! Jo had forgotten to put the lid on the chili pot before he and Gary drove in. They hit a pot hole. There was chili everywhere, all over the back windows and the milk bottles. Then, when they reached the building there was no water. The lead from the building water supply branched, one branch to the Pie Car and the other to the animals. The animal crew had dragged the hose into the building, disconnecting the part that served the Pie Car. They were happily watering the animals when Jo found out what was going on. Poor Jo lost it. The concession people were crowding around looking for food and coffee, but Jo and Gary were past trying to please.

The cold affected the concessions too. "Do you know how much I made yesterday?" asked one of the women. That was Saturday, a three-show day. "$6. That's how much!" In normal weather, she often made $100 on a three-show day. The take had been so poor that Angel hadn't even asked them for rent.

I rode home on the bus with Carlos (Wheel of Death). The poor guy was sick and worried. He looked like hell. The diagnosis was bronchitis and gastroenteritis. I love those 'itis' words. They just mean "inflammation of" whatever comes before. Anyway, poor Carlos was worried that his symptoms indicated a darker and more dangerous origin. The fear of AIDS was prevalent throughout the circus. The old wife-swapping games had stopped. I remember a tall, thin concessionaire running up and down the steps of the arena. He wanted to show how fit he was, how he could still walk the steps and sell the goods. Eventually he went home to his family to die. Now Carlos was worried. He talked of rejection. He probably just had the flu. The poor thing needed mothering. I loaned him my hot pad to cuddle and counseled Tylenol.

We were finally on the home journey. On the train, the corridors were dark. Since we had headed east from Denver, the windows on the southern side had been crudely swathed with aluminum foil sheets to reflect away the light. In the Pie Car, my three companions coughed interminably. The bronchitis virus had swept through the circus. "Here comes the plague train," we joked. In every city we caught the disease of the week and went into sick sync. I pictured my blood as the repository of a vast swelling colony of antibodies, all rich ethnic varieties building up to a mass Coca Cola commercial singing, "We are the world, we are the people." It was not enough to be plague ship USA. The latest troupe of Chinese was itching to infect our bodies with the new improved version of Beijing fever, or the Poles, Rumanians, Bulgarians, Mexicans, Italians, and Germans could be counted on to take a quick trip home and return with some exotic viral import before we could ever achieve that elusive state of wellness.

Finally, we were heading south. We had an engine driver with a southern accent and Polish-born Taddy, our trainmaster couldn't resist trying out his Alabama accent as he instructed the driver to "Hightail it to Georgia."

It didn't work. We were pushed over onto a siding to let other trains past. Eventually Taddy tried the pregnant elephant waiting to deliver story.

This time, the driver responded with a Polish accent. "Okay, okay, we're going to hightail it to Georgia right now."

"Make my day!" proclaimed Taddy. Both engine driver and trainmaster kept calling the dispatcher. Finally came the answer they wanted. "You get green lights all the way."

"You did good," said the driver to Taddy.

"We both did good," Taddy responded.

CHAPTER 12

DOWNTIME

Circus people love to entertain, and they entertain lavishly. They also love to dish the dirt, and circus gossip is so rich, so colorful I'm addicted. Get-togethers are always good occasions for the exchange of gossip. One such occasion was the night of T's birthday party. T was a porter on the train. She was a good-looking African American woman with a great personality. Mr. T, her husband, was the head porter and he had done well by her. There was beef barbecue, ribs, and chicken. Huge mounds of food: salted nibbles, veggies and dips, fruit, nachos, and spicy rice were piled on tables. I sat with Mark who entertained me with the goods on various performers. Apparently the father of one of my students is a whore dog, a shameless womanizer on the cross-country drives between venues. He drives overland and picks women up in bars. Back at the circus train, he treats his wife like a Southerner treats his dog, but that is only when he's been drinking. However, since he drinks constantly, that means often.

Some stories were more immediate, more exciting. I remember one evening when Eddie came running around the front of the train. He had just been scouting around the end of the coaches and spied one of our bigwigs who was around the back of the train getting head from Ava (name changed). Our high-up was busy getting a blow-job from the mother of one of my students. No task is too much to ask of a circus mother. Family is everything! Her daughter had a great act, but with a little help from someone in power, she could have a top act. If you have to give head to get ahead, so be it! I remember trying to show how insightful I was about the ways of the world once while pontificating to the trainmaster's wife. "It's not what you know," I proclaimed, with an air of superior knowledge, "it's who you know." Cindi trumped my ace. "It's not who you know," she came back, "It's who you blow." Obviously she wasn't alone with that point of view.

Before we left Hollywood, I went out with Nicole, drank Margaritas, and learned of the wife-swapping days of the upper echelons: Marco's affair with Marisol, and Eric's liaison with David. David is a charming young alcoholic from concessions. At the last company party in Madison Square Garden, David went as Nicole's date, so that Eric could charm the bigwigs. David was supposed to be drying out. Instead, he got Nicole to pretend that his drinks were hers so that Eric wouldn't kick him out. David is a charmer, but he spends money like water, his own and anyone else's who will loan it to him. That includes me. He owes a fortune to the IRS. They will never collect. What a waste of a potentially great guy!

The major celebrations come at special occasions though. I've never known a Halloween like they have on the circus. We left the building at 10:30, just after the last show. The restaurant was waiting for us. The assortment of costumes was wonderful. There was an incredible lady zebra. Eugenio went as Dracula, David, the clown, as the Hunchback of Notre Dame, and Leshik, our Performance Director, as Napoleon. There was a Cat in the Hat, and a pregnant concession lady came as a cow, complete with rubber udders. Several of the little kids were there. They'd had their own party earlier with food, games, apple bobbing, and visits to the various dressing rooms to call, "Trick or Treat" and collect the booty. Whitney Boger won the kids' prize as a witch with dark green makeup, a long hooked nose, and black talon finger nails. Sebastian went as a lobster; then there was a little mermaid, a great spider, Ninja warriors and a terminator. Casey Boger went as a ballerina fairy and Ned, the runt, went as Mike Tyson. My favorite though was Elvit, who went as an acrobat walking on his hands. Large gloves covered his feet and he had shoes on each hand which he held up in the air. An oversized jump suit covered his head and a mask in front of the crotch area looked like an upside down face.

I went as Marge Simpson. I wore a vivid blue ski cap stuffed full of foam and tied with elastic under my chin. The bug eyes came from an egg carton and the beads came from the dollar store. I had family there! There were two characters in Bart masks.

Bobby Miller, the first engineer from the train crew, stole the show. Bobby was young, trim, blond, and hetero. He went in drag as the "circus slut." He had gone to a lot of trouble and was very convincing. He had the wig, the make-up, slutty clothes, padding where it mattered, and some kick-ass high-heeled shoes. I thought that he was a woman doing a Tina Turner act with the hacked hair and miniskirt. He worked the room, pouting, throwing kisses to the men, and blowing their minds when they saw him heading into the men's bathroom. He'd been active earlier, strutting his stuff before various members of the crews. Chris, from the animal crew, swore that he'd got a date with "her" to the delight of those in the know. The following morning a lot of guys tried to say that they were just going along with the joke. The truth was that Bobby had scored a knock-out. Bobby was pretty confident in his assumed sexuality and gave the come-on signal to a few of the train crew. Not recognizing him, a couple of them figured that they were going to get lucky. Later they vigorously denied their interest. Anyway, Bobby got first prize: a gift certificate to a local department store. The best part was the following morning in the Pie Car. Bobby came in for a lot of teasing. The word was that the prize was a $50 gift certificate from the Gap.

"What are you going to spend it on?" he was asked. "I hear they have some great jeans dresses."

"No," someone protested. "He's got his heart set on a pair of engine-red fuck-me pumps."

Bobby was eager to set everyone straight about the conclusion to his evening. "I stayed away from 45 coach last night," he said. "By the time I'd explained, it would have been too late!"

"Good thing Cowboy didn't see you," offered one of the crew. " You looked a lot better than his last one!"

I love the way these guys kid each other. November 2 was Smiley's birthday. Pete and the animal crew got a stripper for him, with strict instructions not to overdo – just down to a teddy. Poor Smiley was embarrassed to death.

The circus does know how to celebrate. I got three cakes for my last birthday. A couple of weeks later I had two Thanksgiving dinners. The first one was in the Pie Car. They did a great job and judged it to the last slice. Later that night, I went to the Laribles' coach. Eric, Richard the hairdresser, Karen, and a bunch of other people were there to share a twenty-four-pound turkey. There were two kinds of exotic dressing: ricotta, rice, spinach, and almonds; and also sausage, orange and sage. This came with mashed potatoes, gravy, and then key lime pie. The Laribles had made a wonderful antipasto of prosciutto, salami, grilled eggplant flavored with anchovy, olive oil, and garlic. Then there was bread, wines, champagne, and an incredible Italian desert. Vivien Larible, our head-balancing aerialist, probably made dessert. This is her forte when coming on to men.

" For you, only for you, I make my tiramisu," she would say, pouting, exaggerating the Italian accent and batting her long eyelashes at the guy under attack. She makes tiramisu sound like a sex orgy. Nobody stands a chance.

Later that evening, Alyson, a new dancer, gave me a lift to the Gardenia restaurant where Eric, our singing ringmaster, was giving his benefit. Eric has a wonderful voice and raised more than $800 for Equity for AIDS. After the show, we all went to a Japanese restaurant on top of a hill overlooking Los Angeles. It looks beautiful at night. Daylight is a different story – people begging on street corners, crack dealers out on the sidewalk. We lost a lot of crew in LA. I couldn't understand why.

"Why LA?" I asked Tim, our Manager. " It's the pits! Why not San Francisco? In LA there are dope dealers on every street corner, pan-handlers everywhere pestering for money, and derelicts pushing rusting shopping carts full of junk."

"You don't understand," said Tim. "A lot of the men feel comfortable here. It's what they're used to. These things don't bother them. Now, the artsy types, they'd pick San Francisco, but we don't have any artsy types." Gays are common in the entertainment business. They love to perform, but most gays are too fastidious for the circus.

One of my most memorable outings when we were on the West Coast was the trip to Calistoga Springs. A group of the women and I drove down the valley for a day and evening at the mud baths. These were large depressions carved out of the rock and filled with thick wet rotted vegetation, like fine peat moss. We lay in these, covered up to the lips in soggy mush, while I led the group in constant choruses of a song I learned in kindergarten in England. It is the celebration of mud, sung by a happy pig and constantly repeated. It goes

Mud, mud, glorious mud.
Nothing quite like it for cooling the blood.
So follow me, follow, down to the hollow.
And there let us wallow in glorious mud.

And so it continues as the last word, mud, becomes the first word of the repeating verse.

We had all been primed with good California wine before we entered the baths, and soon, all of us were singing the round with enthusiasm, constantly repeating the four-line verse. Eventually it was time to crawl out of our hollow. Our bodies were plastered with goo. Every orifice was filled with mud and twigs. We were ordered to stand against the wall of a large communal tiled shower. Then, our warders turned the hoses on us. What a fun day!

What do circus people do in their spare time? Why, they go to the circus! Several of the circus people told me that they had been to see the Cirque du Soleil in New York City. They also went to the Big Apple

Circus, and would visit any minor circuses we come across. Circus was in their blood. They only left one circus job to move on to another. I remember a visit to Las Vegas a few years ago. My time with the circus was over, but I was still in touch with circus people. Some of our Russian performers were in Vegas, performing in the Cirque there. The son of one of them, a former student of mine, got tickets from his father and invited me to see the show with him. I was amazed as I compared the Cirque performances to ours.

"Look! Look, Taras!" I exclaimed. "Vivien Larible, she could do that," We watched a young woman balancing on her head on a trapeze bar as it circled the stage.

"Yes, Meesees R., Vivien Larible, she could do zat," he responded gravely.

"Look! Look, Taras! The Kaganovich troupe, they could do that," I said, watching an amazing group of acrobats sailing above the stage.

"Yes, Meesees. R. Zee Kaganovich troupe, zey could do zat."

"But the mysticism, the feeling of magic, Taras," I said. "Where does that come from? How do they do that?"

He smiled down at me condescendingly. "Meesees R. Zey do some heavy duty drogs."

CHAPTER 13

DEATH IN THE CIRCUS

Death comes to the circus in many guises. My first experience of this was when Doug, one of our train crew, died unexpectedly. He had experienced poor health for some time, but went about his work without complaint. One day he just failed to show up on time. Later, checking his room, they found him. He was curled up on his bunk. Rigor had already set in and so maneuvering his body out of the small cramped room, along the narrow corridor and out through the vestibule took some doing. Other deaths were more dramatic. One Chinese performer hanged himself. Most people drew the conclusion that he couldn't accept returning to his own country after the five-month visa expired. Who knows? The dead don't give us answers.

How hardened the men are toward accidents. The Assistant General Manager rushes over, forms in hand, so that an accident report can be filled out. Then all seems to be forgotten. In Madison Square Garden, one of the lady flyers fell, shattering her wrist and ankle. Before the ambulance had carried her away, people were applying for her job. In Michigan one year, a young woman was killed instantly after falling twenty feet. The Chinese are the most unfeeling. One Chinese performer fell off the top of the bicycle pyramid as it was circling the ring. His eyes were rolling upward. Two others just picked him up, rushed him to the side of the ring, dropped him and returned to their positions without bothering to see if he was okay. The show must go on!

Flyers frequently have accidents in the circus. Most flyers use an attachment called a safety. Soon after I arrived, a flyer's safety broke and she fell some distance to the floor. She lived, but needed considerable time to recuperate. People were applying for her job before she was hauled out of the building. Desi, a flyer and the sister of one of my students, had married into a prominent circus family. She died during a show when working without a net. Desi's safety broke or was improperly attached. She plunged to her death in the middle of the act. She was a beautiful young woman with a character to match her looks.

The death that affected me most was Bobby. Bobby Miller was the handsome young man who worked as first engineer to the circus train. He was happy, lively, and fun-loving. I particularly remember the Halloween party when he came dressed up as the circus whore.

Life has a way of picking us up and dropping us with no warning. The circus trainmaster was having a torrid affair with one of the dancers. I lived pretty close to the trainmaster's quarters and when the affair started I was the first to know. I could hear her high heels clattering past my door in the evening when she started paying late-night visits. Unfortunately for them, the trainmaster's wife, who had been living back in Florida with their small child, paid an unexpected visit during one of these evenings. She had planned to surprise her husband, but she got more than she bargained for. I heard the fireworks and the scream of, "Get this bitch out of here!" The ultimatum that followed left us minus a trainmaster. Bobby thought he had a chance to get the job, but he was turned down. His pride suffered. He felt rejected and didn't want to take orders from a newcomer. That was a pity because he gave up his job as first engineer with the train and joined the crew who worked at the building.

Sunday evening was the usual time for load-out when we left a city. Bobby was working with the building crew that evening when we were pulling out of the Cow Palace in San Francisco. He wasn't yet familiar with the load-out routine of that crew, and there was a lot of pressure to move fast. He was driving a tractor and pulling one of the heavy wagons back to the train. Turning a corner at an intersection he made an error. The wagon rolled, the tractor rolled, and Bobby was pinned underneath. His chest was crushed by the weight of the tractor.

When Bobby arrived at the hospital, he was pronounced brain dead. It was a dreadful shock to those of us who knew and loved him, but to his fiancé, Diane, a young woman who worked as a porter with the train crew, it was devastating. They were a committed couple. They had planned to get married when they reached Denver. Diane sat by his bed and watched the machines breath for him. She talked as if he were going to recover, but we all knew that it was useless. When the time came to leave San Francisco, she got back on the train. Bobby had ten days on the machines before the plug was pulled. Staying wouldn't have changed anything.

We had moved on over the mountains to Salt Lake City before the package came. Diane got a message that it had arrived and was waiting for pick-up. She knew what it was: Bobby's ashes. Diane had no transportation to get it. I had just arranged to borrow a car to get groceries, so I offered to drive her for the pick-up. I wrestled with myself over the appropriate route: groceries first and then pick up Bobby's ashes while our groceries melted, or ashes first which would have meant leaving them in the car while we grocery shopped. Somehow, that seemed like sacrilege.

I remember that journey from Utah to Colorado – bleached white stretches of barrens, marshy lowlands wet and rank with weed and willow, the rusty tumble of the deciduous trees on the foothills, and the golden splash of aspen against the darker pines. I remember the aspen. I remember Bobby's funeral. The land and the solitude always bring back memories

From Salt Lake City, we traveled over the Rockies to Denver. One engine didn't cut it pulling us over that terrain. Sometimes there were three or more engines coupled together pulling the enormous weight of the elephant herd, the horses, people, vehicles, wagons, and a train more than a mile long. Finally we got there and were met by Julie, a former circus employee who now lived and worked in Denver. She had a car and offered to help. The following morning, Diane, her friend Nancy, Julie, and I piled into the car. We drove into the foothills of the Rockies to a hillside looking down the valley toward Denver. As we climbed the hillside we could see a small gully where a single aspen tree sprouted from the soil, its leaves golden in the sunlight. Diane was clutching the box of ashes with one hand. The first finger of the other hand was hooked into the handle of a bottle of Wild Turkey, Bobby's favorite drink, while her palm clutched a single shot glass.

There are certain ceremonies that we, the living, owe to the dead. Without benefit of church, minister, or casket, we made up our own service. We stopped, grouped around the tree while Diane emptied the ashes around the base. She then poured a shot of whiskey into the glass and emptied it onto the ashes. She fed another shot into the glass, saluted Bobby, threw back her head, drank a toast to him and handed the glass on to me. The bottle did the rounds as we each drank to a young man we had known and loved. Then we made our way down to the small town at the base of the hill and browsed the local tourist shops. I bought Diane aspen leaf earrings for remembrance. She left the circus soon after that. Too many memories!

CHAPTER 14

GUNTHER

Soon after I joined the circus, I met the alpha male. Gunther Gebel Williams, the animal trainer was an impressive man. Five feet four inches tall, with a lean muscular physique and long golden hair, he exuded power! Gunther was born in 1934 in a village in Silesia that is now part of Poland. He saw little if anything of his father, a soldier who fought on the Russian front and never returned to the family. His mother, a seamstress, was left with the task of supporting her two children. At the end of the war, when the Russians had moved into the area, Gunther, then only twelve or thirteen, earned a little money helping the officers take care of their horses. He learned the voice commands that the soldiers used to control them. It is amazing how sometimes a skill or a technique we master in our youth can color the rest of our lives. This skill was to be Gunther's passport to success.

One day the Williams Circus came to town. Gunther learned that they needed a wardrobe lady. He urged his mother to apply for the job. Well, she got it, joined the circus, and took him along with her. Gunther was only fourteen at that time. The plan was for him to hand out programs and help people find their seats while she took care of the costumes. The life didn't suit her, though, and she didn't stick around for long. She quit and left Gunther behind. This could have been a disaster for a young boy, living with a crew of mature men. Fortunately for him, the circus owners (the Williams) took him in to live with them rather than putting him in the tents with the roustabouts. There were two Williams children, an older son and a daughter around Gunther's age, who would become his friends. The daughter became his first wife.

As time passed and Gunther grew older, he started running the horse act. He used the same voice command method he had learned with the Russian horses. Later he took over the elephant act, and ultimately, he handled the big cats. He always used the same technique of spoken commands. He was an impressive animal trainer, soon to be famous throughout Europe. Then tragedy struck! The Williams' son, who was due to take over the running of the circus, was killed in an accident in the ring. Old Mr. Williams had already died. Carola, the wife, now owned the circus and soon Gunther was running the whole show for her.

Gunther added Williams to the end of his name. He was now Gunther Gebel Williams. This was when Ringling heard of him. RBB&B was looking for a new animal act. They had heard about this remarkable animal trainer in Europe – a man who controlled animals with his voice alone while the rest of the big cat trainers were using a chair and a whip. Ringling sent their scouts out to Germany to see if they could lure him away from the Williams Circus. Gunther wasn't having any. He owed Carola. She had been good to him and he was committed to her. The next step for the Ringling scouts was to approach Carola. Ringling offered to buy the whole Williams circus, with the provision that Gunther go with it. This offer was accepted. The old Ringling Circus became the Blue Unit and the Williams Circus, headed by Gunther, was to become a new unit: the Red Unit. Back in the United States, a new circus train was put together. Gunther set sail for the New World, complete with elephant herd, horses, big cats, and men. What a voyage that must have been! Like Noah's Arc setting off into the unknown. A new beginning and Noah was the star of a new show.

Gunther had retired from the ring the year before I arrived, but he was still in charge of all the animals and supervised their care. He had an incredible rapport with them. It was hard to see how the unit could have managed without him. I vividly remember one day when school was about to start in an area where the tiger cages were located. One of the animal crew, responsible for locking the cages, had messed up big time. "Tiger loose!" came the cry over the loudspeaker. I quickly hustled the kids into a nearby restroom. Unfortunately, one of the children, who was not in the classroom area at the time, decided to head for the door to the parking lot. The tiger had the same idea. The exit door, down a narrow short flight of stairs, opened inward and had a small square window at face height. The boy was trapped against the foot of the door when the tiger came running behind him. Fortunately, he was not its target. It was heading for the light and freedom. The cat reared up with its two front paws at either side of the window. It couldn't push the door outward, so it was trapped when Gunther came running to the top of the stair. Thank God that he arrived in time! He coaxed the big cat back to its cage. The boy was saved from the cat, but almost expired from terror. Without Gunther, who knows what might have happened.

Gunther had a big stake in the show. The gossip was that he owned forty-nine percent of the Red Unit. I wasn't surprised. His family occupied one-and-a-half coaches on the train, plus a deluxe bus parked near the arena. Gunther's second wife, Sigrid, went first-class too. She would come home most days laden with purchases from the local high-end shops.

Sigrid still looked good though, a glamorous woman! Gunther had always gone for glamorous women. He couldn't settle for a Plain Jane. He could afford the best. He had first seen Sigrid and her small daughter, Tina, sitting in the audience in Germany years before when he was still performing with the Williams Circus. He learned that she was divorced and he went after her. After the show, Gunther approached her, made a date with her and eventually married her. Gunther and Sigrid only had one child together, their son, Mark Oliver.

For a man as powerful as Gunther, one wife was not sufficient. A mistress was a given, and Gunther could select from the best. Every two years, the circus would put together a new show. This meant an influx of new talent. The dancers were generally the most promising of the newcomers when it came to shape and beauty, but sometimes he would choose from the international group. Gunther would look them over and make his selection. His mistresses were always lookers. Rejection was not frequent. Young performers from countries where women are chattel and life is a desperate struggle considered it an honor to be selected as the mistress of a rich and powerful man. Sometimes they were content to just provide services in the hope of getting some advantage for themselves or their children.

He had his standards though, and as far as he was concerned, smoking was not acceptable. If he saw one of the showgirls smoking, he would walk up to her, pluck the cigarette out of her mouth and step on it. One day in my first year when I still smoked, he caught me smoking outside the building. He walked toward me with hand outstretched, but I stopped him. I held out my hand, palm toward him and said, "If you say nothing about my smoking, I'll say nothing about your sex life." He backed off.

Before I came to the show, an acrobatic act, a group of young girls from Romania, provided some real drama. The man in charge of the act sold the sexual services of some of the girls in the troupe to the working men. Eventually these girls were persuaded to complain. The authorities were brought in and the offending troupe leader was deported. Most of the girls had to leave with him. That was tough, because in those days, even servicing the animal crew was preferable to the lives that some of them had back in Romania. They didn't all go back though. Gunther selected a couple of the best performers to join his family act. Eventually his son, Mark, married one of them. Talent is valued in the circus. Marriage usually means a merger of talent, power, or connections.

Anyway, back to Gunther. He was still in charge of the care of the animals, but he looked too good to be retired from command of the ring. In his black tuxedo, white ruffled shirt, and head of thick gleaming blond hair topped by a black cowboy hat, he drew all eyes as he circled the building on his big black motorbike. He was all-powerful. He dominated the horses, the tigers, and the elephant herd. He moved among them like a king, cracking his whip, slipping food treats into mouths, rewarding with a pat, a word. The elephants revered him. The Red Unit elephants, apart from Congo and Sabu, were all female and Gunther was their lord. Sigrid was seen as a rival. She dared not approach the elephants. She dared not arouse their jealousy.

At this time, Gunther had some minor health problems, including arthritis. He could no longer do the required heaving of props and the gymnastics of the ring on a continual basis. This was a pity, since his son, Mark, was not yet the equal of his father. Mark, the heir apparent, had the tall, stretched-out relaxed grace of America. That sense of barely controlled explosive energy was missing. He ruled through the father's power, but he gave no sense of knowing this. His own power would come, but it was not there yet. He rode the elephants with a throw-away nonchalance. His gestures were no more than choreographed movements: a routine. They said, "I've done the stunt. Now, you are supposed to applaud." Still, this lacked conviction. The sense of danger was missing. Mark made it look too easy. Gunther could not afford to leave until he was sure that Mark would be well established to perform with all the animals before he left. Mark already handled the elephants and horses, but the big cats were a different proposition. Eventually he would have to handle these if he wanted to be the star of the show.

A couple of years later when we did the "Children of the Rainbow" tour, a new tiger trainer arrived. Tyrone was a big, tall African American. He could do the job, but he didn't have the magic. He didn't inspire shock and awe. For one thing, he was too big. He must have been about 6 feet. 4 inches tall. Seen from a distant seat in the arena, he seemed to tower over the cats, making them look small, puny, and nonthreatening. To the tigers he was uninspiring. They went through their routines sloppily, reluctantly. They did what they had been trained to do, but their hearts weren't in it. Occasionally though, Gunther would decide to go into the ring instead of Tyrone. The announcement would come over the loudspeakers. "As a special treat to the audience in this city, Gunther Gebel Williams, the great animal trainer, is returning to the ring for one performance." Gunther would ride into the ring on the back of an elephant, slide off and enter the cage.

The cats, lounging at ease, expecting Tyrone, would suddenly realize what was happening. They straightened up and almost clicked their heels. You could practically hear their thoughts in tiger-speak. "Oh, shit! Look who's here!" Then, there was the effect upon the audience. At 5 feet 4 inches Gunther did not tower over the tigers. Suddenly those cats looked as dangerous as we knew them to be. The effect was electrifying. Suddenly the act was exciting.

CHAPTER 15

CIRCUS GOSSIP

We started the West Coast ascent in Fresno. I got a lift home several nights with Joel, the Blue Unit's trainmaster. Joel's wife, Cindi, was working with me, teaching the small children. After a long day coping with the noise, the clamor, and the craziness, we would be wired. Joel would thrust a beaker into each of our hands. A drink! A drink! A beer was just a beer, but a drink usually meant something of much higher octane. The principal fuel was Absolut and were we grateful!

Sometimes Mark would drive along with us. Mark's girlfriend never made it on the promised visit, but he was over that. A new showgirl had invited him out, so he was up on the hormone high again. What a gentleman he was! There was a torrential downpour one night. The ground in front of my coach door was awash. Mark waded through it, dragged the heavy yellow metal step stool to mid-puddle so that I could stride across, then he waded back to get my stuff out of the back of the truck. I felt like Queen Elizabeth when Sir Walter Raleigh spread his cloak over a puddle for her to walk over.

My coach was pretty close to the clown car, but they were seldom around when I got home. They were usually first at the building in the morning and last there at night. They had to go in early since they did most of the publicity interviews for the circus, and they got out late because it took so much time to remove the disguises. The clowns probably worked

89

harder than anyone. They didn't get much glory. Their primary role in the circus was to divert the attention of the audience while the sets were being changed. If the tiger cage was being erected, or the globe of death was being hauled in, the clowns were out there cavorting and miming for the attention of the audience. Funny, but I found it hard to get to know the clowns. In real life, without their makeup, they faded into the background. They were not outrageous. They didn't screw around, have affairs or show-off in real life. When they put on the makeup though, they wanted attention – they demanded attention. Without the disguise they disappeared. I didn't recognize them.

The wire walkers lived just a couple of coaches from me. They provided good gossip. One week, Ivan, the principal performer, split up with his live-in girlfriend. There was a loud, dramatic quarrel outside the vestibule, as Ivan threw her clothes off the train onto the platform and she berated him for his inadequacies as a lover, as she ran around scooping up her wardrobe. It was most entertaining. There was quite a crowd of us, eager to help with the pick-up chores and get the dirt first hand.

Further back, a couple of the coaches were occupied by our Russian performers. Russia used to have five state circuses. The state supported a large number of performers as they trained, practiced their art and then performed. When the Berlin wall came down, this system fell apart. The performers had to find employment elsewhere. Our scouts rushed over and snapped up some great acts. The sudden move to the West must have been frightening to some of them. We were the big bad capitalists. One day, soon after their arrival, as I was walking alongside the train, one of the Russian women gave me the sign to avert the evil eye. She extended her arm with the palm forward and the first and little fingers up, while the second and third pointed down. I've not been struck down by a bolt of lightning yet, so obviously, the devil does not yet have me in his grasp.

In the evening the Russians were more relaxed. They loved to sit out alongside the train on their folding chairs with their food and drinks. As they made money, they bought cars and spent their time polishing their new purchases. When they were not drinking vodka or polishing cars, they were fishing. If there was a ditch or a waterway alongside the train, the Russians were there, reeling them in. The problem with this was that they liked to dry them and make fish jerky. The best place they could find to do this seemed to be in the air handlers. Fish jerky is considered a delicacy. The fish were gutted, then opened up. The carcasses were salted, seasoned, and slipped into the ceiling channels. Of course, the Russian coaches stunk of fish.

In Hollywood we had a Girl's Night Out. We were out till 1:30 at a downtown bar. The margaritas were great and Mara, the national publicity agent, picked up the tab for about ten of us. The search for the perfect margarita continued. I sat with Kimberly, one of the showgirls. Wow, did she have the goods on everyone. Her own short history with the circus was interesting. Dave, the blond gypsy guy from Concessions, gave her a whirl and she ended up dumping him. He retaliated by calling her the n word. He wanted to tell her how great he was, what a stud he had been, how she was small potatoes compared to him. He didn't like being her reject. This is typical though.

The showgirls usually look down on the concessionaires and working crew guys. They seem to think that the performers are some kind of royalty and that, if they attach themselves to a performer, they will be moved up the circus social ladder. It doesn't work like that though. Showgirls are for playing around with, not for marrying. Of course, there can be payback for this. One dancer reputedly gave the crabs to the whole of the Kaganovich Troupe.

Los Angeles! What a city! Piccolo's little motor bike was stolen. Piccolo was a chain-smoking German-born dwarf who came over to the United States with Gunther years ago. Monday morning, he went to the A&P supermarket across the street from the sports arena. He left the bike outside while he went in, and when he came out it was gone. He was mad as hell. The problem was that the same thing had happened to him months earlier in Venice, Florida. With a bike that size, a thief doesn't need the key. He just picks up the bike, throws it into the back of his truck, and takes off.

The crew seemed unsympathetic. "He should know better. That shop is in a bad district." After a drive around, they all seem like bad districts. This city was full of doped-up panhandlers who could turn nasty. Wherever we went it was, "Got any money?" "Got any change?" That didn't stop our guys though. A crew member got on the bus last night with beer. He had risked life and limb to buy it in that neighborhood. The other guys started teasing and sneaking six packs out of his cardboard box. He retaliated with, "Don't make me kill again!"

The following day, back at the building, Piccolo's bike had already been replaced. It was probably Gunther. Gunther used to get mad at Piccolo, but Piccolo was a part of his youth, a part of the Williams Circus that took in a teenage kid and made him into a star. The little kid's motor bike that fitted Piccolo initially had a washer to cut back on the throttle and make it safe for kids. The washer was removed in the shop, and soon, Piccolo was zooming again.

On Sunday we had an early start. Sunday is generally the last day in a city. There were two performances at 1:00 and 5:00. I caught the last bus to the arena at 11:30 a.m. The last bus was always an hour-and-a-half before the first show. I watched the first part of the performance where Tina fell from the top of the arena on a bungee cord. It bounced her back just before she reached the ground. We called this trick, "The Stockbroker's Special" – advanced training for the Wall Street crash. Kathy, one of the other women, did this same act a few years earlier. There was always a catcher to help steady the jumper when she landed. The catcher for Kathy was a boyfriend who had been cheating on her. Somehow, when she bounced back from the ground, she always managed to kick him in the teeth. He tried to dodge, but she got him every time. It was a performance that never failed to entertain the girls.

Thank God for the little heater Tim loaned me. The AC was freezing my bones. I'd tried stuffing socks in the vents. I wore a sweat suit, wooly nightie, and bed socks, but I was still chilled to the bone. I couldn't imagine why the AC was so savage. I think that the trainmaster had the control for our coach in his rooms. Maybe he was burning off his nightcaps and needed to cool down. Still, with a heater set at 80 to fight the AC, I was doing nothing to solve the energy crisis, but I would survive.

CHAPTER 16

ARIZONA

I love this part of the United States. We usually arrived in Tucson first, when we came down from the North. There is a great national park just outside Tucson where millions of years ago, before man had evolved, a giant meteor hit our planet causing clouds of dust to fill the sky. Darkness covered the earth and some say that this led, ultimately, to the death of the dinosaurs. I always took my classes to that particular site when we were in Tucson. From Tucson we would move on to Phoenix with its outdoor cafes where mists of water cool the air and make it possible to breathe. Phoenix is a city where things happen. One of those things was the big day off.

We had quite a show from the buses that morning. It was just daylight. One of the showgirls, Karen, was doing her warm-up stretching exercises on the flats. At first, I thought it was our crazy showgirl, the one who goes skipping and clicking around the circus, as if she is hard wired to her Sony Walkman. This was quite a different performance though, totally unselfconscious. Everyone on the bus turned to watch the perfection of the routine, the rhythmic warm-up, repetitive bouncy dance steps, the stretches outlined against the rising sun and the aching, burning, small leg circles and lifts from the horizontal. My whole bus was silent as we watched.

We were all off to the Salt River. Last year this outing was organized for the first time, but only a few people went. It was supposed to be one of those cultural outings arranged for the Chinese, but this year everyone got in on it. Last year, one of the circus guys who was staying at a nearby hotel got drunk and drowned in the hotel pool. This time though, there would be no accidents. It was going to be fun. We would float down the river on inner tubes. Buses would drop us off upstream and pick us up downstream an hour or two later. We would float past cliffs and hills dotted with huge cacti, bob over mini rapids, and swirl around whirlpools. One little problem was the choice of tubes. Those who arrived early got big substantial tubes: 18-wheeler tubes that could hold a bunch of people. The latecomers, the ones on the last bus, had to float down the river on bicycle inner tubes. I was on the last bus. Thank God I can swim!

Ned sat beside me on the bus going there. He was small and runty for his thirteen years. His parents had unloaded him for the day on Teresa, the trainmaster's wife, but she wasn't exactly hovering over him. The parents were mad at him for something and were threatening him with all kinds of terrors: poison and killers who would get him if he got lost. The stepmother was really angry at him. She had recently lost a child, a boy, in a miscarriage. Ned is the child of the previous wife and was the living proof of the stepmother's failure. Poor kid! It was hot and he was dressed too warmly. Still, I was thankful that I was wearing a long-sleeved blouse and pants. The sun was blistering.

One of the showgirls, Tara, broke out in a rash when she got in the river. After getting out of the water, she passed out. Rick told Steve about it later.

"She was out cold. We carried her up to the concession stand and laid her out on the table. When she came to, she couldn't remember anything. She thought she must have walked up there herself."

"Good thing she wasn't with the train crew," remarked Steve.

I wonder what he meant by that?

It was good to be back in Arizona, close to the Mexican border. The scenery and the wild life are unique. The desert vegetation next to the building was home to all kinds of animal life. One morning as I entered the building I saw some large, strange-looking lizards sitting on the shoulders of a couple of the guys. They were the neatest looking creatures with a crest of points over the top of the head. These were great horned lizards. I had to admire them. They were impressive. "Do you want one, Teach?" asked one of the crew. I thought about it. I would look so cool with a great horned lizard on my shoulder, kind of like a desert pirate with a parrot substitute. "Sure," I said. "I'd love one."

"Okay, we'll catch one for you," he promised. "Just stop by tomorrow."

The following day as I entered the building, he called me over. There was a cardboard box sitting on a table. He opened it and pointed. Inside was a great horned lizard, but it lay motionless on its side. It was pale and flaccid. I poked it. It didn't move.

"Is it okay?" I asked.

"Sure," he said. "It's fine. It's just cold here in the building. When you get it back to the train it will warm up. It'll be all right."

I thanked him and took the box over to Pete, the stable boss.

"What do you think, Pete?" I asked.

"Teach," he said, "you have one dead lizard there."

Still, I didn't want to believe Pete, so that evening, when I returned to the train I sat the box on my desk on top of a hot pad. I also got a bowl of water, lifted the lizard's chin and placed his jaw on top of the edge of the bowl. I figured that he might need water and that if the heat revived him he would have the water right there where he could get it easily. During the night I got up several times to look in on him, but there was no movement. The following morning I faced facts. My lizard was dead. Just because I had wanted to look cool, I had caused the death of an innocent little creature. I didn't want to just drop him into one of the trash bags hanging from the side of the vestibule. I decided to take him back to his home, to the desert area where he had been caught: the dry arroyo bordered by sage brush, which skirted the building. I found a big Tupperware container and placed him inside. With the container and a large digging spoon in my bag I took the early bus to the building.

I planned my own little service. When I got off the bus, I climbed over the fence and went down to the dry stream bed. I knelt down in the gravel, set the box on the ground, pulled out my spoon and, mustering a state of mind appropriate to the conducting of a funeral, I dug a deep hole in the sand. Then, I put down the spoon and lifted the lid off my box. There was a blur of movement. The lizard jumped right out of the box and zipped away into the sage. That little bugger had been playing possum all the time. I made my way into the building and told the guys what had happened.

"Don't worry, Teach," they said. "We can get you another one."

"Don't bother," I replied. "They're too smart for me".

It was in Phoenix that I had my back surgery. I had been lifting heavy supplies from the school box for a long time. My back was killing me. I had been to a doctor and chiropractor in a couple of cities, but they didn't help. In fact, the pain was getting worse. I was in agony. Tylenol and Advil wouldn't cut it any longer. I needed relief. One of the dancers, Gunther's current mistress, was helping me. She sat by my bed and made sympathetic noises as I rolled in agony. "Go to the musicians," I begged. "They must have drugs." Instead, she went to the trainmaster. Taddy phoned ahead. When we pulled into Phoenix, an ambulance was waiting for us.

The ambulance crew scrambled onto the train and hauled me off the coach on a stretcher. As I crossed from the train to the ambulance I saw the huddles of people watching my exit. This time I was the gossip center. I was the drama queen. In no time at all, the Pie Car would be buzzing with the details of my dramatic exit. I was quickly slotted into an ambulance, and whisked off to hospital. I had chosen the hospital because I knew the lab director, a family friend from my old life. He was waiting. He advised me to ask for a particular doctor, a neurosurgeon who specialized in back injuries. The next couple of days passed in a drug-induced trance. I was scheduled for keyhole surgery for a ruptured disc. After surgery I remember being visited by a group of guys from the animal crew. They examined my chart with interest. Drugs were their subspecialty.

"Teach," said one, with the air of someone knowledgeable "They're giving you some good shit."

The circus train moved on without me. Fortunately, I had contacts. As soon as possible I was released from hospital and went home with my lab director's ex-wife. I lay on my bed of pain at her house and prepared myself for a long horizontal visit. Unfortunately her air conditioning did not cooperate. The temperature hit 100 degrees and we escaped to a nearby hotel. I had soon had enough. I booked a flight and spent the whole trip swinging by my forearms above the seat. I did not want to put any weight on my spine and screw up my patched disc. Back home my daughter was waiting at the airport with a station wagon so that I could lie in the back and be transferred to my own bed.

It was a couple of months before I could rejoin the circus. I shuffled around my block on daily walks, waiting to feel healthy enough to fly out. Finally I was okay. I flew into San Francisco and was met by Bonnie, a fellow circus teacher. I had been replaced by a stand-in during my absence and Bonnie was so glad to have me back that she kissed the ground I walked on as I deplaned. Shortly we were at the Cow Palace. Jimmy, the Pie Car cook, was on duty. Jimmy was a long-haired ex-hippy. He was waxing lyrical about a return to the gutter and the bottle. He said he planned to look for Officer Robinson, the woman who had brought him down.

"She gave me a ticket once for J-walking and she turned me on. She did it to me! She drove me to it! No, no, the Pie Car did it to me! I'm going to look for a good street corner and a bottle of Thunderbird. I'll survive. I learned how in LA. I can build a regular palace out of cardboard. How many floors do you want? You want a kitchen? A guestroom? Knew a guy in LA. He had a three-story. His old lady walked out on him though. Said she was going upscale: moving up into the corrugateds. I can survive! I'll lie under a car and drink the antifreeze. I'll give blood! No, I can't do that anymore! I've had hepatitis." He considered his options for a moment and brightened up. "I know. I'll give someone else's blood. You get $2 for referring someone." He was on a roll, but eventually he ran out of steam, came down to earth and noticed me standing there.

"Hi, Teach," he said. "Good to have you back. What'll you have? Turkey sandwich? It's on the house," he announced. He hand-slapped the turkey slices between two pieces of bread and handed it to me. I remember noticing that his eyes looked a bit yellow, but I didn't think much of it at the time. When we, the company, were told that we all had to have gamma globulin shots to prevent hepatitis, I figured it out. Still, we were all fine and so was Jimmy.

The circus was quick to arrange the hepatitis shots. Everyone was to be treated. Not everybody was okay with this though. Some people have big problems with needles. We lined up around the circular corridor and shuffled toward the nurses and the shots. One of the boys from the Chicago Kidz act was with me. "They're not going to stick me," he kept repeating. "They're not going to stick me." The closer we got to the front of the line, the louder he got. "They're not going to stick me!" he yelled. When we got alongside the nurses he was in full cry, shrieking, "They're not going to stick me! They're not going to stick me!" at the top of his voice. The nurse tapped him on the arm. "Honey," she said. "I already did it."

Soon I was back on the train. How good it was to be back. The sights, the sounds, the people were so good and familiar. The train is home.

CHAPTER 17

MUGGED IN MEXICO

Illegals are a fact of life in the circus. Whenever we crossed a border, either into Canada or into Mexico, we would lose people. They didn't dare go through customs. When we returned, our people would be waiting for us. Life with the circus was infinitely better than what most could hope for in their own countries. Sometimes they were able to legitimize their status. An American, one of the pyrotechnic guys, married a girl from Russia. They had what we called a green-card wedding. Green-card weddings were pretty common in the months just before the end of a tour. The fact that Jack was gay didn't make him any less desirable as a marriage partner. All that was necessary was his signature on a marriage certificate and his agreement to maintain the fiction whenever the immigration people came calling. Pictures were taken regularly of the happy couple together in different cities as we toured the United States. The truth was that she was shacking up with one of the concession guys and my gay friend was – well, who knows what he was doing?

But back to crossing the border. The circus went to play the *Palacio de los Deportes* (the Sports Palace) in Mexico City one year. It was great! The train went into Mexico with just the stock cars. The coaches with the living quarters were left behind in Houston. Instead of traveling by train, we flew into Mexico City and stayed at a downtown hotel. What luxury! Comfortable beds, room service, breakfast of choice – what more could we ask? The lower level concession people stayed behind in the States. Our core salespeople went in though and had to hire locals to help them. Of course, it was important that they hire Spanish speakers. Not that it made much difference. Our junk was too expensive and the audience didn't buy much of the stuff we sold. The concessionaires almost starved. Still, the job must have looked promising to the new helpers, since we were no sooner back in Houston, than they turned up looking for work. I didn't see how they could have the right to work in the United States. They weren't exactly essential to our economy. I mean, sellers of snow cones and candy floss can't be crucial to any nation, but Mike, our concessions boss, wanted them. He disappeared for a couple of days. I think he flew to New York. When he returned, there were green cards for everyone. It's amazing how quickly our government can move when there is a need. Go figure!

I had been to Mexico a couple of times before, but I wasn't prepared for how much it had changed. I took a group of the circus women to see the Floating Gardens of Xochimilco. I had visited them in the past and remembered them as a paradise of flowering islands where Mexicans and tourists relaxed in colorful boats and watched the landscape float by. Instead, I found a rotting fleet of painted hulks so crowded that salesmen with cases of goods jumped from boat to boat trying to sell their wares. It was sad. The Mexican economy had gone down the tubes. People were desperate and petty crime flourished. The Mexican police were not be found when a crime was going down on the streets, but whenever the take from a Walmart or a bank was being loaded into the local equivalent of a Wells Fargo Truck, a mini army of police, complete with machine guns, was there to guard the money. Police protection was for big business. Ordinary people had to fend for themselves.

I was robbed in Mexico City. It was the high spot of my visit. I had remembered a great downtown flea market with an incredible variety of things for sale. I remembered one guy with a row of baby owls perched along the length of his arm, another clutching a giant mermaid carved out of a tree trunk. The stuff for sale there was so exotic that I couldn't wait to get back. I persuaded Pam, our lady bus driver, to go with me. She had misgivings, but I was confident. "We'll be fine." I promised. "Not to worry!" Still, she didn't entirely trust my judgment as she showed me her new backpack with every zipper secured by a tiny lock.

"Nobody is going to get into this," she vowed.

Now, the Mexican metro was designed by the French. It's a good system. There's nothing wrong with the metro. The problem is with some of the people who ride it. We did fine on the first train. Then we had to change onto a second train. The station platform was pretty crowded and we were swallowed up in a sea of humanity. The train that arrived was also crowded beyond any reasonable limit. We would have preferred to wait, but we had no choice. We were jammed up to the platform edge when the train rolled in. Then we were pushed onto the train by the mass of people behind us. The seats were all taken, so we stood like sardines in the vestibule between the sliding doors.

The train set off. Pretty soon it was evident that I had a problem. I had a very friendly guy standing behind me. His hands were all over me and he was bouncing on me from the rear. I was so wedged in, that there was nothing much I could do. I did realize though, that the real target was not my irresistible body, but the contents of my wallet. I held my forearm tightly across the top flap of my bag. I looked through a sea of heads for Pam. She was plastered against the wall next to the doors. From the expression on her face, she was going through something similar to me. At our change station the doors opened, there was a giant hiccup and we were ejected. We staggered out onto the platform. The train rolled away and suddenly we were alone. Pam held up her backpack. "Oh my God, I can't believe it," she moaned. The bag had been slashed into ribbons. All her stuff was gone. I examined my bag. It was leather, but it had been slit up the side and the contents removed. Fortunately I had lost nothing more valuable than a Spanish English dictionary. My money and credit card were in a money belt under my clothing. Pam was not so lucky.

We were no longer in the mood to go shopping. We switched over to another platform to go back to the *Palacio de los Deportes*. Venders, with goods arranged on blankets, bordered the platform. As we stood there I noticed that one of the venders was selling razor blades. How's that for free enterprise? When we got back to the building the animal crew was particularly entertained by my story of the affectionate mugger. From then on, when I walked around the passages of the building, they would come up behind me, prod me in the lower back with the handles of their bull hooks and say, "Remind you of anything, Teach?" Melody, the young woman who took care of the horse tack, was wonderful. She sewed up the side of my bag with her heavy-duty sewing machine. It's a great looking repair. I love it! I still use that bag and smile whenever I see the stitching.

By the time we had our farewell bash in Mexico City, we had quite a collection of stories. The drummer had been driven into an alley by his cab driver, who pulled a gun on him, took his wallet, and encouraged him to move away quickly by firing the gun near his feet. A performer had been relieved of his wallet by a drag queen in a back-street bar. Events like this were so commonplace that at our farewell party we had a group photograph taken of everyone who had been robbed, standing with our arms around each other and smiling for the camera.

CHAPTER 18

THE BUFFALO ACT

"April is the cruelest month." At least, that's what T. S. Eliot says in his epic poem, *The Wasteland*. Well, April can be the cruelest month in the circus. April of the second year of a performance contract is the month when performers find out whether or not they will be rehired for a second two-year term. Now, every two years, the circus puts together a new show. Every other April, the acts that want to stay on with Ringling have to get a facelift. To be selected to remain with the circus, an act has to change; there has to be something original about the performance, the performers, and the costumes. The act is then evaluated by the creativity team.

If the new act is judged suitable, that means two more years of security. If the changes are not sufficient or the act does not fit in, when the tour ends in December, it is history. This is a time of great anxiety for the performers. With job security gone, they have to hustle. Finding work for an entire act in an international workplace is not easy. It is also a time of great anxiety for the teacher. Angry disappointed people often look for someone to vent on. The teacher is an easy target. In April, it is wise to lie low. Dodging the lynching parties can be a full-time job.

Today, I waited in Kathy's trailer for the 10:00 p.m. bus. The Bogers had been rehired for another two-year stint, so their trailer was a safe haven. The buffalo act was to be renewed. Who could imagine a circus act built around buffalo? I always picture these animals pounding across the plains of old America pursued by a posse of Indians. The very idea of getting them to perform in a circus ring seemed absurd. Still, it could be done and the Boger family did it well. Now, the act wasn't entirely made up of buffalo. There were three buffalo, one longhorn steer, two horses and a pony. Still, the most dangerous animals were the buffalo and I stayed well away from them.

This act was put together by two brothers, Steve and Rick Boger. These were both family men who traveled from city to city with wives and children, driving or towing their animal collection overland as we moved from city to city. Steve and his wife Kathy had three children, Chris, Casey and Katie. Rick and wife Pam had one child, Whitney. I got to know the Steve Bogers pretty quickly. When I arrived at the circus, two of their children, Chris and Casey, were already in school, but the parents soon let it be known that they wanted me to take their youngest, five-year-old Katie, into the early class. Previously, five was considered too young. Age six had been the cutoff. I had my doubts at first, but I was soon converted when I realized that they were prepared to string me up by my thumbs if I refused. Fortunately, Katie was a bright little girl. The advantage to me of teaching three of Steve's kids was that it made me almost part of their family.

Soon I was hanging out in the Bogers' trailer and dining on Kathy's cheese dip in the evenings, while I waited for the circus bus to take me back to the train. It was funny to see their animal trailer parked out on the street with the big longhorn's head poking out through the side window into the street, horns sweeping half the length of the trailer. Also, I didn't want to leave and miss the excitement. The Bogers had two new little mountain lions. These were purchased from a breeder as cubs and had arrived by plane the previous day after a six-hour flight. The airport people didn't know that these were mountain lion cubs; they just thought that they were large kittens. The long-term plan was to incorporate them into the Bogers' Buffalo Act for the next season. The cubs were spotted like Bambi and spent most of their time sleeping, but the moment they awoke, they squeaked urgently with hunger, like baby birds.

As usual, Kathy was multitasking. "Here, take this," she said, thrusting a baby bottle into my hand as soon as I arrived at their trailer. The bottle was short and the contents were thick. "What's in it?" I asked. "Food," she responded curtly, grabbing a squealing kitten and thrusting it into my arms. Boy was he hungry! He had been sucking on the other kitten's umbilical cord until it looked raw. Now, it was time for the real thing. Kathy grabbed the other cub, then a second bottle, and we both plugged in our charges. The bottles contained a mix of yoghurt, pureed chicken, baby food, formula, powdered calcium and iron salts. The nipples of the bottles had big cross cuts. Those mountain lion babies latched onto the bottles and sucked them dry in no time flat. My cub knocked back two and a half ounces in about thirty seconds, then fell back, unconscious. Kathy's cub did a repeat performance. Then they lay back, dead to the world, and slept until the next attack of hunger pangs awoke them.

After a feed, they were okay for about two hours. Kathy had to feed them constantly through the night – plus wipe their rear ends with wet tissues to program them to void their bowels. "In the wild, the mother usually licks their rear ends to produce this effect," said Kathy. "I'm not willing to go that far." The next morning I saw Steve buying donuts at the Pie Car. "Home cooked breakfast?" I asked.

"She's too busy feeding the kittens to give me anything," he complained.

Those mountain lion cubs matured fast. They could soon poop unaided. In no time, Kathy was giving them their first bath in strawberry-scented shampoo and they were heading for the kitty litter. Later, I saw the baby tigers and mountain lions leaping around outside the trailer in separate cardboard box playpens. The sight of those big heads and tiny bodies whirling around was fantastic. They were going to need lids on the playpens soon. Those mountain lions could climb! They were as cute as can be though, as they dived for meat scraps. They slunk around, bellies to the ground, trying to look like fierce little hunters. They adapted well.

When I left the building late Saturday evening I came across Steve pulling Pepe on one of those retractable leashes. Pepe had just been declawed. I could see the red dots where the claws had been extracted on his front feet. It didn't seem to bother him though. All four paws were in brake mode. "You've got this all wrong," was the message. "I'm a rugged individualist. I'm not supposed to do this walking routine." He was slimming down a bit. The fat tummy was going, but the baby Bambi dots were still there. A couple of weeks later I saw Steve and Pepe out walking again. This time the roles were reversed. Steve was being pulled by Pepe.

Now, whenever we went into Canada, half the concessionaires stayed behind. Maybe they were illegals or were wanted by the police. Who knows? Rick Boger, Steve's younger brother, was perfectly legal, a good old boy from the South with an animal act. He just had a bad memory. He'd forgotten to bring his ID. The organizers were panicked. Three of the acts depended on him. The Canadian customs officials grilled him for a couple of hours, then one of them said, "He's got to be an American. Can you see an illegal trying to sneak into Canada with a longhorn steer in the back of his car?"

What a practical joker Rick is. I was a prime target for him with my English accent and my proper image, plus, I could always be counted on to react beautifully. Walking toward the building in Phoenix I tiptoed along the boardwalk in front of trailers and came across a huge shiny pile of dog turd. Now, the trailer owners tend to have large dogs, which are great deterrents to would-be robbers. Still, finding this pile of poop right in my path did not thrill me.

"Disgusting," I exclaimed as I edged fastidiously around the pile. "What kind of an animal could have done that?" I said, cringing satisfactorily.

At the sound of my voice, Rick came out of his trailer. Gauging the situation, he bent down, picked up the turd between his bare fingers, examined it carefully, raised it to his nose, squeezed and sniffed.

"Don't think it's dog," he said, with the air of a poop connoisseur, as he lifted it to eye level. "Too big for that!" He lowered it and sniffed again. "Certainly not poodle," he judged. "not even Doberman." He gave it one last squeeze and appeared to consider. "Could be train crew!" he announced, sliding it into his pocket.

I was staring at him in horror when he cracked up. Finally it dawned on me. I'd been had by the plastic poop trick. That shiny turd was straight from the joke shop.

Rick had pulled the same joke on Gunther the previous night. He had dropped the poop right in front of Gunther's doorstep, just as Gunther was heading into his coach.

"That goddam dog has all the building to go in and it shits on my doorstep," he roared. "Lisa," he yelled. Lisa had a motor home in the same area, complete with large Doberman guard dog.

Rick appeared out of nowhere. "Don't worry," he said. "I'll pick it up."

"No, I'll get…"

"No problem," said Rick, picking up the offending article, dusting it off and putting it in his pocket.

He didn't tell me what Gunther said next, but from his smug expression, it was very satisfactory.

CHAPTER 19

THE CHINESE

My first experience with Chinese circus performers was in Madison Square Garden. I had just finished my job interview with Tim, and I needed to use the ladies' restroom. I went into a couple of stalls before I selected one, because several of the toilet seats in the performers' area were split down the middle. Apparently the Chinese performers could not get used to sitting on the lavatory seats as Westerners do. In China they commonly use "Squatty Potties": holes in the floor, to squat over when voiding. Anyway, to get into the same pooping position in a Western toilet, it was necessary first to stand on top of the seat, then crouch and let go. The result, inevitably, was a split seat. Sitting on a seat that had been split by the Chinese took some adjusting, to avoid getting terminal bottom pinch.

Accommodating the habits of different cultures is a constant challenge in an international circus. The Chinese cultural differences were always fascinating. First, there was the weight maintenance. Acrobatic performers have to be very weight conscious. Chinese performers were seen retching over the wash basins in the Garden on a daily basis. They may have had flu, but the more likely explanation was bulimia to keep their weight down. I once taught two young Chinese girls who did a contortion act. Now, pizza is the downfall of the weight conscious. Soon after the girls discovered pizza, they would come to class smelling of vomit. Weight maintenance had started. Then, of course, there was the problem of unwanted pregnancies. The one woman, one child edict of China had to be maintained outside their country. When birth control failed, the girls seemed to expect management to arrange an abortion for them. Apparently these problems were easily handled in China.

Anyway, the Chinese act was amazing: fourteen performers on a bicycle in rings one, two and three. They were spread out, standing on shoulders in an inverted pyramid, their silver, turquoise and yellow costumes glittering like giant peacock tails. It was hard to equate these polished performers with their image on the circus bus, self-consciously examining their recent purchases, usually sun glasses and electronics. They had a knack with the high tech stuff. Most people on the circus train had televisions with bunny ear antennae. Moving from city to city and trying to get decent reception was always a challenge. The Chinese solution was incredible. They would take a coke can, cut off one end, snip a zigzag pattern of cuts around the open end, and peel it back like a sunflower. With a couple of studs and wires attached to the untouched end, they got amazingly good TV reception.

When we performed in San Francisco, the train used to be parked on the edge of Chinatown. The last time we were in the city, we were told that the tracks had been torn up, so we couldn't park in the same place anymore. Wrong! The tracks were still intact. The rumor was that the circus was afraid that the Chinese troupe might disappear if we parked too close to Chinatown. The solution was to keep them close to the train. Fortunately this location had entertainment to offer. A creek ran alongside the track, close to the train. It was swarming with crayfish. The Chinese love crayfish. It's hard to catch them in the daylight, but out in the darkness with flashlights, you can scoop them out of the water by the handful. Another Chinese defected in LA. Bob says that the Chinese usually defect in San Francisco. One year, the circus lost thirty out of a troupe of forty-five.

The Chinese usually came in on short-term visas. Apparently, the group is changed every five months. Maybe the authorities back in

China didn't want to give them time to adapt, learn the language, and be seduced away by our Western ways. Nothing could stop this happening though. They were a fascinating group of people, but we never really got to know them. The sheer size of their group and the language barrier kept them in their own miniworld. They travelled with their own government-approved translator who was also changed at regular intervals. A couple of times a week, when they went out to the bowling alley or to buy beer, they had the bus to themselves. They remained a people apart. They never came to the Pie Car, since they had their own cook. They also had their own cockroaches. They stored their food in open containers in their coach and provided a constant challenge to the debugging squad.

Toward the end of their time with us, performers would start to disappear. Their three bicycles, one in each ring were soon pared down to two bikes, one in ring one and the other in ring three. Later, when these peacock tails also became embarrassingly short, the circus had to settle for just one bike circling the center ring. As this tail too was pruned by even more defections the troupe was reduced to using the studious lady interpreter to peddle the bike.

Still, every time we saw Chinese performers at the back stage telephones we figured that they were planning to defect. What happened to these defectors? Did they all become waiters in Chinese restaurants? We had a couple of Chinese lady contortionists who disappeared around this time. The rumor was that they'd gone to work in a brothel. China has made such progress in today's world that it is hard to imagine the motivation of those performers who dreaded returning to their country. One performer hanged himself in his room. You have to be pretty short to hang yourself in a room on the circus train. The ceilings are low. I imagined him, short and slim, clad in the sparkling costume of the Chinese performer, swinging slowly.

The schoolroom held a fascination for the Chinese performers. It was not unusual to host an influx of them, looking at the maps on the walls and trying out their vocabulary. One day they descended on us spinning plates on handfuls of thin rods, like bunches of spring flowers.

They were attracted by the celebration that was going on. At lunch, that day, there was a birthday party for Alex. She was six. All the little girls wore Hawaiian skirts made of bright tissue paper. The grassy slope beside the building was covered with people, tables, food, and decorations. All the Chinese turned up. They had a problem with the language. When one got the message that he was invited somewhere, twenty-nine clones arrived with him.

Interesting that even interpreters can have problems with the language. I was teaching backstage one day when the new translator dropped by and asked me suddenly, "Teacher, can you loan me a rubber?" "Good God," I thought. "What does he think I am?" Suddenly, my mind clicked back to the vocabulary of my youth. "Eraser!" I exclaimed, realizing that he had learned British English. "In this country you say eraser!"

CHAPTER 20

THE BIG CATS

Soon after I joined the circus, I watched the second part of the five o'clock show. At first it seemed like the usual fare. During the intermission, the clowns had diverted the audience while the big cat cage was assembled. The lions and tigers filtered into the ring and went through their routine with Marco Peters directing. They leaped around on tubs in the center ring, surrounded by a pitifully weak-looking circle of chain link fence – low enough, I thought, for a determined cat to scale. Outside the ring, two special tigers, Caesar and Bimbo, waited in small towing cages for their performance.

After the main cat act, Marco left the ring and was joined by his brother, Phillip. Caesar and Bimbo were released from their cages and padded across the ring on leashes, led by the brothers. Unbelievable! Two tigers on leashes! One tug and they could be ripping up the audience. But no! The men led their cats into rotating drums at the end of the arms of a huge pivoting wheel. The next few minutes sent me into shock as the two men, blindfolded and dressed in skin tight suits of white satin, straddled the tigers as the arm spun faster and faster around its fulcrum. It was quite an act.

When the train parked in Harrisburg, the capitol, about twenty-nine miles from Hershey Park Arena, the tigers were parked outside the entrance to the building. Marco was pulling the extension cages from the sides of the containers when I arrived. The Bogers, who have the buffalo act, had their mobile home parked slightly downhill on the sloping parking area. That was a problem. When Marco hosed out the cages, the tiger urine flowed in their direction. According to Steve Boger, "Tiger piss will eat the numbers off billiard balls." The lions were just beyond the tigers, next to the building. As Marco was manipulating one of the cages, a lion backed toward him and sprayed urine all over him, marking him as lion territory. "You fucking bastard!" shrieked Marco, as he rushed away to shower.

A few weeks later, as I was walking toward the building one morning, I noticed Marco standing by the cages. I was used to seeing him in the ring clad in his tight white satin suit and looking like God's gift to women. This day he wore blue jeans and a ratty T-shirt. He was setting up a table outside a wagon and hauling out a hindquarter of beef to carve. With a huge knife and a saw he was slicing a thick steak off the end of the quarter. He cut it into four pieces and started to score the surfaces. Then he pulled out a box full of bottles of worming powder. He sprinkled this liberally onto the meat, then rubbed the powder into it. That was why the surface was being scored! The wet groves hold the powder. This is done every three months I learned.

I moved closer. "They eat pretty well," I commented. "What happens to the prime rib?"

He grinned. "Well, sometimes they get it, but then, at other times, they have to put up with Feline Chow."

Feline Chow is a mixture of ground meat and various unmentionable types of offal. It comes in big plastic tubes and doesn't look too appetizing. If Feline Chow is on the menu, Marco plunges his fingers into the mush and sprinkles the powder into the depressions.

"Even large cats can be finicky," Marco commented. "Two of the cats won't touch the Feline Chow, so we always have to buy meat for them."

One thing is for sure though – the cats never go hungry. Nobody wants to find himself in the ring with a pride of hungry lions.

Suddenly it was time for feeding. Philip strolled up. Marco let me go between the cages with them to watch. This is the only time that the cats are separated. Barriers are put down between the cages. With this precaution, they can't fight over the food. Philip used a stick to hold up the flange at the bottom of the cage. Marco knew when to stand wide and sling the meat in underhand for the grabbers, or when he could push it in by hand for the polite cats. He knew which ones he could trust and who to watch out for. Earnest couldn't be trusted. Earnest is a grabber. Sometimes I saw a giant paw poke out to claw at the food. The pacing and cage banging subsided quickly as the cats all got their meat. Then, the separating doors could be opened as first hunger was satisfied. There had to be an afternoon show for them to be fed so early. Timing the feeding is essential. If they are fed too late, they eat so much that they don't want to perform; too early and Marco starts to look tasty. I noticed that one of the cats only got half rations. "She won't work if she is given all her calories on show days," Marco explained. "She just goes to sleep. Before the train ride she gets extra fat to make up for the missing calories."

Baby tigers were born after our arrival day in Phoenix. The first one was born about 6:00 a.m. The mother carried it about for a while, but then she seemed to lose interest. Those cubs would be a nuisance to bottle feed if she rejected them. Two more were born in the afternoon – so tiny. Marco had closed the cage up to give them privacy. The lions were leaping about like maniacs, crashing against the bars. The smell of the blood, the afterbirth, gave them the idea that it was feeding time. Now that the cubs were here, there remained the question, "Who is the father?" There were three males in the group, but they had all supposedly been castrated. Who would be sued for child support? If anyone needed child support it was Marco. He had the cubs in his trailer and they were tearing his place apart. I dropped by to see how things were going and ended up with a bottle in my hand.

Another of the tigers was pregnant. This one didn't belong to Marco. No more surprises were wanted. If she gave birth while the others were around, the kittens would be killed. Only Caesar and Bimbo belonged to Marco and Philip, so the new kittens, if they survived, would be the property of the trainer who supplied the mother.

Years later, when I worked with our twin circus, the Blue Unit had a trainer from England. Graham had paid his dues handling cats in Europe. His family was in the breeding and training business in England and provided the cats that Graham handled – large impressive lions. These were not soft, easy, little beasts. They were the real goods. They looked like huge females, but they were castrated males who had lost their manes along with other more intimate parts. They demanded a tough vigilant trainer who could face up to trouble. Graham got it early in the tour. We were in Birmingham when the lion attacked him. During a training session in the building, one of the cats was giving trouble. Graham was focusing all his attention on the offending animal when another lion moved in from the rear. The attacker had been waiting for his opportunity and sprang. He got his jaws around Graham's back and was shaking him like a terrier with a rat. Tony, a big blond guy who had come over from England to take care of the cats, went into the ring with a crowbar in his hand. He slugged the lion until it let go of Graham and then dragged him from the ring. Graham's parents came over from England to visit him in hospital. They presented Tony with a necklace of tiger teeth as a thank you gift for saving their son. Tony is quite a hero in my eyes.

I asked Tony why he had chosen to go into the ring with a crowbar instead of a gun. "Think of it!" he said. "The cage is a ring of chain link. There are all sorts of people around the cage. If I shot at the tiger, the bullet might go through him and hit someone else. I couldn't take that risk."

It was a couple of weeks before Graham returned to the ring. The doctors couldn't sew up the wounds right away. Lions don't floss. Their teeth are seething with bacteria. The meat in their diets rots as it sits between the teeth and any wounds they cause can become infected quickly. Better to let the wounds drain their poison before sewing them up. Graham was in the hospital for more than a week. My students made some pretty original get-well cards with lots of drawings of great big cats chewing up tiny little Graham. They did say "Get Well Soon" though.

For the rest of that two-year tour, the circus tried to give away the lion that had attacked Graham. It couldn't be destroyed. Lions are a protected species in this country. Unfortunately, a castrated male was no good as far as zoos were concerned. Nobody wanted it. For the remaining eighteen months of the tour it had to be housed and fed. It never went into the ring again; it was far too dangerous. At the end of the tour, Tony took some of the lions back to the breeding farm in England. He packed enough meat to keep them happy on the return sea voyage, which was a good thing, since the trip took four days longer than anticipated. Any further delay and he might have had to feed them a steward.

When Tony returned, I enquired about the fate of the attack lion. "How is the lion?" I asked.

"Dead," he replied.

"What did he die of?" I enquired.

"Heart attack," he replied.

"That was sudden," I commented.

"Yes," he responded. "It happened about thirty seconds after the bullet hit his brain."

Tony had brought back tigers for the new act. These were no better than the lions. They were trouble! Graham's brother, Richard, arrived with them, ready to participate in the new act. He had raised two of the new tigers from cubs and was very attached to them. I was not present in St. Pete when the next incident occurred. Graham and Richard were in the ring rehearsing the new act. There was no real audience present, but there was a photographer taking flash photos for publicity and one or two spotters, including Tony. Cindi, the trainmaster's wife, gave me her account of the incident.

The tigers were agitated by the flash photography. Graham's brother was leaning forward and kissing the head of one of the young tigers he had reared. The other tiger was jealous. It rushed forward, took Richard's head in his jaws and crunched. Richard lay in the ring in a pool of blood. Graham had seen it happen, but could do nothing to stop it. The guys opened the door from the performance cage to the exit. While Graham held back the tigers that were milling around smelling blood, Tony entered the ring and dragged Richard out. Graham signaled the men to open the door leading to the tunnel exit to the holding cages. One by one, he guided the tigers to their exit and out of the ring. All of them, that is, except for the attacking tiger. That one he left in the ring while he went to his dressing room.

A short time later he came back. He came back with a gun. He walked into the ring, marched up to the tiger and emptied the chambers into its head, yelling, "Take that, motherfucker. See how you like it. Take that, motherfucker, take that!" Graham will never perform in the United States again. His brother will probably never lead a normal life again. The damage that tiger did to his brain is not reversible. Such is life! Such is the circus.

CHAPTER 21

THE BABOONS

The baboon act, a colorful and unusual act, belonged to the Stevens family. Lee Stevens – tall, lean, and blond was circus from way back. Judy, his wife, was a first-generation performer: relatively new to the life. Lee had met her at an Audubon Society Reserve in Canada where she worked with the birds. Now, after several years of marriage, they had two cute little boys, a troupe of baboons, a small herd of miniature ponies, a Great Dane, and a macaw. I saw pictures of Judy in her old life. She had dull, light brown hair and washed out features. You wouldn't have given her a second glance. Marriage to Lee had transformed her. She had acquired glamour. The original meaning of glamour was a magic aura. In Judy, this spelled out as bleach for the hair, inch-long artificial eyelashes, and high heels with fishnet stockings.

As the assistant in Lee's baboon act Judy looked terrific, but in truth, she was purely cosmetic: nothing more than a good-looking cheerleader. However, Judy had her own small pony act. Dressed as a cowgirl, she urged her little charges over their hurdles like a glamorous dominatrix. The ponies were further encouraged around the ring by a huge black and white dappled Great Dane called Blueberry, who followed them over the jumps and chewed on their tails.

Lee's act was the standout, however. A group of female baboons, dressed in bright-colored tutus, cavorted around the ring at his command, walking the tightrope and jumping across large wooden drums, which Lee would roll and reposition quickly during the act. Judy would make the styling gestures that say to the audience. "Aren't we wonderful? You can applaud now!" Unfortunately, one year, the baboon act had major problems. While hauling the heavy equipment, Lee ruptured a disc in his back. He was in agony and needed surgery urgently. There was no way he could continue to perform, but there were still bills to be paid. There were payments to be made on the big wagons that carried the baboon troop and the ponies. There was the cost of the feed, the vets, and the transportation cost to get them from one venue to the next. If the act didn't continue, the money would stop. There was only one solution to the problem. Judy had to take over Lee's act as well as her own. Now, baboons are very hierarchical. The troop had accepted Lee as the alpha. Judy didn't have this status.

Baboons are ugly vicious animals. We are not talking about cute little monkeys here. We are talking about primates with jaws that can crack bones and tear holes out of flesh. Now, periodically in the wild, female baboons have menstrual cycles accompanied at times by a large dose of PMS. You can imagine what PMS will do to a baboon troop, since a group of females living together tend to cycle to the same calendar. Not only would they have hair-trigger tempers, but their bottoms would swell to enormous proportions so they couldn't fit into their tutus. Usually, as we zigzagged around the United States, Lee could get local vets to prescribe drugs to combat this situation. Injected periodically these kept the buttocks from terminal inflation and the ladies from going into melt-down mode. He always kept these hormone shots in good supply, because if, at an inconvenient time, the baboons cycled into a PMS phase there would be big trouble. This had happened once in the past when Lee couldn't get a vet to supply what he needed. And, as if facing a troop of baboons with PMS wasn't bad enough, Judy cycled in sympathy. Lee couldn't even go home for refuge. Judy was waiting to hit him with both barrels. He was determined that this should never happen again so he kept the drug supply high. Still, there was the alpha status problem.

Baboons know exactly where they stand in the pecking order. They know who is number one, two, three, and so on, but the status order can change daily. One evening, out of the blue, number four might suddenly decide that she can take out number two and move up the ladder. Since this status envy was a frequent event, every so often, when the baboons went back to their cages, Lee would remove the dividers from between the cage sections and let the girls get at each other. It was a time to settle scores and move up or down the social ladder. After a quick free-for-all involving large bites of flesh ripped out of targeted individuals, a new ranking would be established. Fortunately, baboons heal rapidly. It was important, however, that this readjustment never happen in the ring. Now Judy was going to have to handle all of this.

One bright morning Lee moved out. He sat in a wheel chair with a big white macaw on his knee. The two kids pirouetted behind him, excited to be flying out and going to Grandma's. Lee was off to the airport and the care of distant doctors. His parents would take care of the kids and the bird. It was important that Judy have no more responsibilities. Two acts were enough to cope with. I moved off the train and into the trailer with Judy, to keep her company and act as a quasi-chaperone. Of course, we were not alone. For additional protection, there was Blueberry.

When he was not performing, Blueberry hung out in the AirTran trailer with us. Blueberry took up a lot of floor space. When we sat around in the trailer, he lay between us like a big dappled rug. He was calm, peaceful, and easy on the eyes. There was one little problem, however. He was not easy on the nose. He would lie on the floor, his eyes looking into space, as a cloud of gas would leak soundlessly from his rear end, filling the trailer with noxious fumes. He remained the picture of innocence. "Not me!" he seemed to say. Who else could it be? Judy? Me? We would run for the door as soon as we breathed the first fumes. It was a good thing that nobody smoked. If that gas cloud had ignited, it would have blown up the trailer.

It was important that Judy have no more responsibilities. It was also important that she have company. I quickly realized why Lee had asked me to move in. Judy was just too glamorous. The dyed blond hair and the inch-long artificial eye lashes certainly attracted the animal crew. Occasionally there would be a knock on the trailer door. One of the guys who took care of the horses could always find some excuse to stop by. Still, Judy had enough to keep her busy. She didn't need any extracurricular activities to add to her stress. Carrying the two acts and organizing the care and transportation of all the animals was enough to cope with. One evening, while she was rolling and repositioning the drums in the ring, one of the troupe made her move. Judy came out of the ring that day with blood pouring from a major bite on her leg. One of the ladies had decided that she would take on Judy for the alpha position. It only happened once. Judy got tough quickly.

That night she left the trailer and went into the wagon with the holding cages. I understand that she grabbed the leg of the offending baboon, and pulled it through the bars. Now, she had its attention. Exactly what form of reasoning she used must have been very effective. After that, she had no more trouble. Judy was now queen of the baboon troupe.

CHAPTER 22

THE ELEPHANTS

Elephants fascinate me now. In the Red Unit, we had a herd of twenty-one. There were only two young males, Sabu and Prince. Most were Asian and female. Congo was the only African elephant. She was a spectacular animal with huge ears and long tusks capped in silver. They were so bright that I wondered if the animal crew used silver polish on them. Congo was a forty-year-old with a tricky personality, maybe even a sense of humor. To a new handler this could be pretty frightening. One new guy said that she came up to him and butted him till he fell over. She then leaned over him with her tusks on either side of his body. Fortunately, her ears were back, flattened against the sides of her head. With elephants, when the ears are forward and outstretched, making the elephant appear larger, it indicates an angry, threatening mood. It's the opposite with horses

Chris gave me the elephant's names in order of line-up. There was Asia, Dame, Tonka, Luna, Sita, Rhani, Peggy, Mary, Chichi, Nelly, Zara, Banana, Asan, Baby, Ziam, Blunko, Jenny, Rolli, Tobi, Congo, Prince, and Sabu. Apparently Ziam used to be close to Sabu in the line-up, but she attacked him a while ago and the order had to be changed to separate them. Of course, Sabu probably brought it on himself. He's pretty young though. Little Prince, who was mothered by a surrogate, was also showing a nasty streak at times. He would let people approach from behind until he could stretch back and kick them. The three female adolescents didn't give the same trouble as the young males.

Most of the elephants were old, although four new ones had been added recently. By old, I mean in their fifties. The normal life span of an elephant is sixty years. Sabu was one of the youngest and a troublemaker. Sabu had already been gelded to cool his temper, but it hadn't worked a hundred percent. Dr. Houks was the one to castrate Sabu. Castrating elephants is a real job. The testicles don't drop. They stay in the body cavity, so the elephant has to be anesthetized, then cut open to remove them. That must have been quite a procedure. Still, his performance can't have measured up in entertainment points compared to the Russian guy who came to castrate a bear a few years ago. I was told that this guy brought along a frying pan, then cooked and ate the gonads (aka Rocky Mountain oysters) while they were still warm.

Dr. Houks is a frequent visitor to the unit. He is the veterinarian for both Red and Blue Units. The elephants had not been well recently. The hay must have been off. Hay is bought and shipped in from local farms, but not all sources provide good quality. Several of the elephants had diarrhea and Asia was off her food. Normally they get a variety of food: about ten pounds of sweet feed grain plus apples, bread, carrots, and hay, but nothing tempted Asia. Her neighbor wanted to lean over, giving sympathetic strokes and twisting trucks. Asia wasn't having any though. She was at the end of the line and leaned as far away as possible from the rest of the herd. The vet was called.

One morning I walked by to see Dr. Houks standing on a tub with his arm (up to the arm pit) in an elephant's rear end. He was scooping out the poop. Whether the elephant was impacted or our vet was feeling for polyps I don't know, but it was a sight to behold. That elephant poop is quite a prize. It is much sought after by avid gardeners. I saw an elderly man staggering off that day with a metal tub full. The circus offers it free as grade A chemical-free fertilizer. A newspaper article brought in the organic garden buffs with their buckets. If the size of the turds has any relationship to the size of the harvest, there would be some monster squash and tomatoes later that summer. The advantage to the circus is that they don't have to pay the cost of a dumpster to carry the stuff away. They might consider getting rid of the tiger poop with a similar pitch. I hear that foxes will not cross a line of tiger poop. Chicken farmers should jump at the stuff.

The best place to shovel huge quantities of elephant poop is just outside the ring as the elephants wait to go in for their act. Before they go in, they have to get into line and stand on their back legs with their front legs on the back of the elephant in front. It's like a chorus line. The weight of the turd pressing on the rectum triggers wholesale pooping. The building crew guys rush up with snow shovels and fill the buckets. It's best to do this before they go into the ring, as this line-up is also part of their act and the audience doesn't need to be treated to the sight of a whole elephant herd plopping poop all over the ring.

One day I took the 8:30 bus back to the train. I sat next to Rick, who smelled strongly of elephants and looked sweaty and unkempt. He said that he'd been feeling depressed. His long distance romance was cooling. Telephone calls to his girl were being fielded by the father. Rick hung around today to help Dr. Houks medicate the herd. This is not a straightforward proposition. Getting medicine into an elephant takes stealth. The elephants watch what is going on, and if they see medicine being poured into their drinking water they are capable of tipping it over. To dose Asia, Rick would put the medicine into apples and then arrange to have the apples appear to fall accidentally while he was passing close to her. She figured that she was stealing them and crunched them down. If the elephants think that their bread or apples contain pills, they manage to eat them and spit the pills out.

What a sight those elephants were early today when I arrived at the building! They looked like raccoons. The skin around their eyes had been oiled and had darkened. After the oiling, it was time for a pedicure. Their toenails looked cracked and yellow. That's one of the drawbacks to a life spent walking on concrete. One of the animal crew told me that he once saw a small circus where the vehicles were parked on raw land on the outskirts of town. The elephants in this circus walked on grass and dirt. Their feet were in great shape and didn't need constant attention. Anyway, Gunther and a helper manipulated huge files, sawing away at the toenails of the elephants who stood patiently with one foot up on an elephant drum. Cascades of white powder came showering down. I don't know if this has an aphrodisiac effect, but Sabu, in spite of just being castrated, had a huge erection. I noticed the same reaction on a couple of the horses.

When elephants get ill on the road, imagine what could happen! If an elephant dies, how do you move the body? Where do you bury it? There was nearly a fatality with Peggy in Phoenix. Mary started feeling mean-tempered in the night and butted Peggy so hard that she slipped and hurt her leg badly. She couldn't get up. Preston, who was in charge, woke up Pete, the stable master. Then Pete sent for Gunther. Gunther was unfazed. He had the chains cut to release Peggy from the line, then, with a combination of a bull hook to encourage and a bar to lever, he eventually got her on her feet. It took a half hour and she only got up on the third try. There was a possibility that the leg was broken. Peggy was taken out of the line and moved next to Sabu. Fortunately he was in a good mood!

Now, what would have happened if the leg had been broken? She would have had to be destroyed: shot probably while the rest of the herd was elsewhere. The body would have to be dragged out of the building. It would be impossible to get a crane inside the building, but one would have to be stationed outside to lift the body onto a flatbed. Then the flatbed would be driven to some distant site for burial. The hole would have been dug earlier, using backhoes and bulldozers. What expense and what organization that would take and it would have to be done fast! A live elephant smells pretty bad: a dead one in one-hundred-degree heat would be no bed of roses.

What our elephants needed was a good river to wade in. I wonder how the local farmers would respond if they saw an elephant herd wading in their river. I doubt if the elephants would ever come back. Now that we were in warmer climes, at least, they were getting washed. Today, they stood out in the yard in the sunshine. Minus chains, they waited patiently for their turn to be hosed down, then to stand in the drying line. Poor Asia, she needed to get better. She had lost 800 pounds. Weight Watchers would be proud! Sita, on the other hand, had no problem maintaining her weight. Even her paralyzed trunk didn't stop her getting food. She used a swinging motion to sling the food-laden trunk up to her mouth. The circus people do their best to take care of the animals, but there are limits to what they can give.

When it comes to elephant stories, one of my most stand-out memories of Birmingham, Alabama, was when Jimmy Silverheels came to visit. That year, I taught the small children in a specially designed school wagon. It was carried on the flats and then towed off into the train yard or the building yard. When the two units, Red and Blue, circled the United States, there were occasions when the circuses were relatively close together. On these occasions, the circus folk with transportation would often visit each other. Now, the Red Unit had the largest elephant herd, but the Blue Unit had the largest elephant. This was King Tut, an enormous elephant who was so tall that he could not be contained in a stock car on the train. He had to be transported in a massive truck, driven by his caretaker, Jimmy Silverheels. One day, Jimmy decided to come to visit the Red Unit. I was in the school wagon with about eight of the little kids when they heard that Jimmy had arrived. They were so excited! King Tut was the biggest elephant in captivity.

"Can we go see King Tut?" they begged, jumping up and down with excitement. "Can we go see King Tut?" How could I resist such an easy field trip?

"Sure," I said. "Let's go ask Jimmy."

We walked together to the big truck where Jimmy was standing. We asked politely if we could see his charge, and Jimmy was happy to oblige. As I stood there with the line of eight little ones at my side, he reached out and slid back the side door of the cabin. I was watching the children, when I noticed their demeanor change. They started to elbow each other and giggle uncontrollably. I looked up. At first through the darkness inside the cab I could just see the head of the elephant with one red, rolling eye looking out at us. Then my eyes went back and down. All I could think of was that King Tut must have been surprised while reading the elephant version of *Playboy*. Sprouting out from under his belly was something that looked like a tree trunk. My jaw hit my chest. I was speechless. The kids started to laugh out loud. Jimmy suddenly realized that something was up. (Sorry for the choice of words, but I couldn't resist.) He scanned the row of observers, then spun around to look inside the cabin. Abruptly he spun back to face us, straightened up, and announced proudly, "I taught him everything he knows!"

CHAPTER 23

THE CLOWN

I saw the opening again today. The great glittering parade slid silently into the darkened arena, until that wonderful moment when David Larible, the Italian headliner clown, scooped the spotlight into his cap and flung it into the audience. It was a stunning, spectacular opening that never failed to captivate the onlookers. It was also an unusual role for a clown.

Clowns are a different breed in the circus. They are supposed to be funny, but for the majority of clowns, the principal function is to distract the audience while the scenery is being changed for the next act. The headliner clown is a rare bird and David is one of these. He was famous throughout Europe. He had won the Silver Spoon Award there: a very big deal.

David is an outstanding performer. The audience adores him. Typically, he sports a red nose, and dresses in a Chaplinesque outfit of baggy suit plus oversized shoes. He has an incredibly funny routine where he calls on a volunteer from the audience. The great thing is that this is truly an innocent observer, not a plant. The routine involves knife throwing. This is not made clear before the stooge is selected, brought into the ring and manacled to an upright board. David's father, Eugenio, clad in tuxedo, stands by to assist as David prepares to throw the first knife. The stooge is horrified to see David winding up to hurl a knife at the first target area, just above the right shoulder. A blindfold is tied around the eyes of the victim. There is a roll of drums from our little orchestra. Suddenly, the lights dim and the music announces the release of the knife. Eugenio steps forward and stabs a duplicate knife into the designated spot, accompanied by a loud thunk.

David quickly hides the knife he was supposedly about to throw. The audience roars in approval. The blindfold is removed and the horrified victim sees the knife poking out of the board alongside his face. Subsequent throws go to the other side of his head and both sides of his body. After each pretend throw, the blindfold is temporarily removed so that the victim can see where the knife has arrived. The final throw is supposedly to the area between the guy's legs, just under the privates. Poor guy! He is allowed to imagine the worst. After the final drum roll, when Eugenio has stabbed the last knife into place, he is released as David struts around the ring to enormous applause.

On rare occasions, the circus will have its own show. This is a collection of performances only for circus people. A variety of them volunteer to perform. A concession worker might elect to sing. An acrobat might attempt clowning. David performed for us once with an act that had us rolling in the aisles. He pretended to steal a duck, which he had to hide from the owner. He slipped it down the front of his trousers. He had neglected to fasten the zipper and the duck, which had rather a long neck, kept trying to get out. The act was a bit too ribald for the regular American audience, but we had low-grade taste. We loved it.

David was preparing a video in his spare time. He planned to send cuts of various acts to his friend, Sergio, a ringmaster in Italy. He also wanted to keep him awake by adding porno inserts. He approached Eric, the Ringmaster. "Eric, do you have any porno videos?" He explained why he needed them. Now, Eric is gay. He wanted to help, but he had his reservations. "Well, there is this small problem, David. I do have some porno videos and you are welcome to borrow them, but what you want are great big cocks and tiny little pussies. Now what I have are great big cocks and.."

"Oh sheet," said David, backing out of the room.

David, like the rest of us, has his leisure-time activities. He loves golf. Now, Rick Boger from the buffalo act also loves golf, and little Arturo loves golf. Arturo is a midget clown from Argentina. He comes from a very prominent and wealthy family in Argentina, but since he is a little person, he feels more at home in the circus and had been with us for a long time. He is well liked and accepted as one of the guys. In every city where we stopped for more than five minutes, he, David, and Rick would jump into a car and head for the local golf course. David and Rick had regular clubs, but Arturo had short little clubs to suit his physique. After a long day on the links, the three golfers would sit around and rehash the days play. One day, after a hard round of golf the three were sitting together outside the Bogers' trailer. David, pencil in hand, was totaling up the scores and working out their handicaps. Little Arturo couldn't wait. He had to know.

"What's my handeecap, Daveed?" he demanded. "What's my handeecap?"

David looked up, exasperated. "Y'er a dwarf, Arturo," he exclaimed. "Y'er a dwarf!"

Mama Larible, David's mother, had her own problems. Mama was supposed to be cutting back on the cigarettes. She got four a day and had no way to hide it when she went over the limit. I saw her on the corridor one night, trolling for a nicotine fix. At that time, I still smoked, so I gave her one of mine and offered more. There was no way anyone should leave this building for minor purchases. It was too dangerous.

We pulled into Boston on a weekend. Boston is a great city for field trips. I loved to take the kids to the ship, *The Constitution*. I got to tell the story of how she was saved from the wrecker's yard with money raised by the schoolchildren of the United States. The ship was destined for demolition when the poem, "The Constitution," by Oliver Wendell Holmes captured the hearts of the children with its dramatic lines. The poet felt that a vessel that had done so much for the nation, should not be destroyed, but rather, given a Viking funeral.

133

Nail to the mast her holy flag, set every threadbare sail.
And give her to the god of storms, the lightning and the gale.

Boston has so much to offer the visitor. I was so impressed by the history of this city that I encouraged everyone interested to come along on our outings. They learned some titillating facts, like the popularization of the word, hooker, from the Civil War's General Hooker, who arranged for these ladies to service the troops. He is reputed to have said, "If they don't f--- they won't fight."

Anyway, David came along with us one day as we walked around the city. We stopped in front of the monument to Samuel Adams, a very striking monument. David was unimpressed. "Big deal!" he sneered. "What he do? He make beer!"

CHAPTER 24

THE CHICAGO KIDZ

In 1993, the circus put together a new show featuring performing children. We had quite a cosmopolitan group. There were children from China, Mexico, the Ukraine, Bulgaria, Kazakhstan, and Mongolia. In addition, there was a wonderful group of young performers from Russia. The Berlin Wall had just come down and Ringling saw a big opportunity. The USSR used to have circus training schools where talented performers were nurtured to perform in the big national circuses. The new order of the day was private enterprise, so the national circuses were dissolved, and the performers had to find a market for their talents elsewhere. Our scouts rushed over and picked up some great acts.

The Russian children had a skip rope and tumbling act that would fill ring one. We needed a similar act in ring three to balance them. What was needed was a home-grown American act. What we got was a group of African American kids from Chicago, the Chicago Kidz. Now, the Russians were a wonderful act; they were technically perfect but they were not crowd pleasers. They were puny and pale. They gave no drama to their performance. The Chicago Kidz were the complete opposite. Technically, they were not perfect, but the dark lithe bodies in the day-glow costumes, the flashing white teeth, the expansive gestures – these were crowd pleasers.

These kids were mainly school dropouts from a well-known project in the city. They had started performing for handouts on the streets of Chicago. Their act was a mixture of tumbling and hip hop. A local do-gooder had discovered them and tried to make something of them. He trained them, polished their act, and took them to local clubs to perform. From there, they graduated to performing in sporting events at half time and eventually, they came to the circus. The kids mostly had single mothers who were probably happy that their sons got this opportunity. They got to travel, get an education, perform, and earn a good living. What we got in exchange was a class act and a collection of delinquents.

The years we had all the child acts were unusual for the circus. Previously, I had been the only teacher and would have between fifteen and twenty-five children. Suddenly, there were about seventy-five children needing an education. The circus hired three more teachers. The Mexicans, the Chinese, the Bulgarians, the Mongolians, and the Russians – these were no problem. These we could handle. They were good students, grateful for the education they were offered, but the Chicago Kidz! They were trouble! They were a good act, but they had major attitude. Some of them could get violent and confrontational. They were in our faces. One of them would put his face just a few inches from mine and start with the insults. "You'z old. You'z ugly. You'z a whore. You'z an alcoholic." He was looking for pain and if he pressed the right buttons and found it, he was going to keep pressing. Insults were the least of our problems. When we were in San Francisco, a man turned up at the circus train carrying a gun. He said that one of the boys had raped his daughter. We figured out which boy he was describing and made sure that there was no confrontation. The boy was not yet fifteen, but it was rumored that he already had a child of his own back in Chicago.

When these kids came on board, the high-ups – the suits – were delighted with themselves. They figured that they were saints, saviors, heroes. They had saved these children from a rough life on the streets. Unlike the other children, the Chicago Kidz were given special treatment. They had their own trainer, with a van to drive them around. They were each given a new circus jacket, and then the suits came to have their photos taken with them. This accomplished, they handed the Kidz back to their teachers. We had to deal with the problems.

First of all we tested them academically to see what we should order for them from the correspondence school we used. When the books came, the boys were indignant. They were not about to do baby fourth-and-fifth grade work! They demanded higher level work. The supplies we had purchased cost around $500 per student, but these had to be scrapped. The circus gave in and paid for new sets of books. Soon, the boys found that the work was too difficult for them. Next, they blamed the teachers for being unable to make them understand the material. "I cain't do this work cause you'z a no-good teacher," I was told.

Thank God I didn't have to handle more of these kids. I usually taught the Russians and the higher grades. I did have one of the Kidz in my regular class, an older kid, one of the best of the bunch. He qualified for high school work. I ordered books for him from the American Correspondence School. He eventually graduated with a high school diploma, the first in his family to do so. Occasionally though, I would stand in for one of the front-line warriors or admit one of their students to my class on a temporary basis. I vividly remember the first day I got D. (I'm just going to refer to these kids with initials.) D was hell to deal with. One day, he got mad at another student in my class, so he picked up a heavy staple gun and flung it at his victim.

After class I went to the new manager. This man was another of our social do-gooders. He leaned toward me over his desk and in slow pedantic tones, as if he were speaking to a dummy, he pronounced, "Mrs. R., if you...respect them... they...will respect... you." Somehow that advice failed to impress me.

"Sorry, Mike," I said. "I can't handle this kid. If he gives me trouble again, can I bring him to you?"

"No problem," he said. Well, a couple of days later, D had another major meltdown. I hauled him off to Mike.

I waited hopefully as Mike took my problem behind curtains for a heart-to-heart. There was a low buzz of voices, then D's voice emerged loud and clear. "Motherfucker!" He yelled. "Motherfucker!"

Next came an even louder voice: Mike's. "You're fired!" he yelled. "You're fired!" and then, realizing that he didn't have the authority to do this. "Do that again and you're fired!"

One of the major problems for the teachers on this tour was the challenge to be politically correct. One of my shortcomings was that I used to refer to the Chicago Kidz as the Chicago boys. I was told that I was being a racist. I ask you, racist? What is racist about referring to a group of boys as boys? If I were calling a grown man "Boy" to his face, that, I could see, might be misconstrued as racist, or if he were white, derogatory. But to call a boy a boy, what's the problem?

My education in the politics of racism came at a meeting in Atlanta. I don't know what the meeting was about, since we teachers were lied to about its purpose. We thought that we were having lunch with a woman who was an expert in intercultural dialogue. This lady would help us by giving us pointers in how to manage a culturally diverse classroom. What a scam! Whatever the woman's agenda was, it was not interracial teaching strategies. During the meeting several questions were posed about teaching situations. She didn't even attempt to answer. The whole meeting smelled like an NAACP trial of Whitey.

The confrontations started quickly with my use of the term "Chicago boys." Putting that aside we tried to get our expert to give us specific pointers in how to avoid the insults and confrontations of recent weeks. She just told us that we would always have attitude from this group because it was normal for them, and anyway, we white females were the last type of people to be dealing with kids of this background. They would respond much better to black women as teachers, she told us. Black women teachers would get less attitude. It was obvious that she thought the sisters should have our jobs. I got mad.

"Well," I said. "They are going to have to change that attitude then, because I can't change the color of my skin."

From then on there were no holds barred. She asked us what particular problems we had been experiencing. We let it all hang out, from the likelihood that T is a psychopath to D's brain being fried before birth by his mother's drug addiction. I gave examples of R's sick attitudes. I told of the two occasions I had seen him become violent, attacking another child at a birthday party, and an incident in Miami when he attacked a townie. I told of the constant insults intended to hurt and humiliate. I told of the look of delight that appeared on R's face when he felt that he had struck a nerve – had caused pain.

The working men at the train usually stayed away from the boys. They knew that if one of the kids had a problem with anyone, the whole group would back him up. One of my other students got into a fight with one of the Kidz one day. Five of them jumped him and roughed him up pretty thoroughly. They acted as a gang. Well, this gang, it was rumored, was getting drugs from somewhere. The suits arrived to have a heart-to-heart with them. We teachers were required to sit with them as they were lectured. Somehow we were responsible. How can you have responsibility when you have no authority? The Kidz were onto us. The teachers had started off with a school van, but this was taken from us so that the Kidz' trainer could drive them around. The Kidz would sail by in our old van, chauffeured by their coach, while we rode the bus with the animal crew. There was no use complaining. We were last in the pecking order, the bottom of the food chain: plankton!

CHAPTER 25

GOODBYE TO THE CIRCUS

Not content with terrorizing the other children, the Kidz were sharpening their teeth on one of the teachers. Miss Mary (name changed) was the butt of their jokes. Excuse the expression, since it was her butt that was being attacked. It started with M drawing on the white board. He drew a picture of a huge rear end, labeled it Mary and drew a huge penis next to it - also labeled. When Mary let the boys know that she was upset and embarrassed by the drawing, it encouraged them to continue. This time it was A and N who were the artists. Our company manager took a picture of the art in an attempt to document the behavior and get the boys to apologize. D, of course, refused. The request got him running off at the mouth.

"Fuck you, I ain't doin it," he said. "She an alcoholic, an ugly bitch."

Mike lost it and yelled, "You're fired!" again. Well, that firing lasted all of a few hours, so we were still stuck with the little sicko.

Frank, one of the working men told me of his attempt to defend Mary. He tried talking to D. "Hey, man," he said. "Why don't you quit giving that teacher such a hard time? She's only trying to help you get an education"

"You shitting me, man," retorted D. "You just tryin to git into her boody."

"You know what?" said Frank. "He was right too."

Live and learn. Now, if I could only figure out what a boody was. It's probably her backside, ass, bottom, or whatever the favorite term is. Certainly the guys fixate on it. One of them was commenting yesterday on a particularly juicy rear end.

"I wanted to bite her ass and get lockjaw in the worst way. Let her drag me around."

In class one day, Mary felt someone grab her buttock. She turned to see L. "Did you touch me?" she demanded.

"I wouldn't touch that nasty thing," retorted L, grimacing in feigned disgust. The Kidz were always taunting Mary about her weight. R would squeal like a pig to get the class all worked up whenever Mary turned her back. What could she do?

Well, the Kidz got worse and worse. One of our nicknames for this group was the Teflon Delinquents. What we meant by that was that nothing stuck. Two of the boys, D and R could both be classified as mentally deranged. Both of them had been fired and sent back home, but when the ring started looking bare, the firings were rescinded. Eventually they pushed it too far. D was hauled off to jail in West Palm Beach for throwing rocks at a police car. Two of the Kidz actually tried to rob the Pie Car. How crazy can you get? For these little incidents they got KP: shoveling out the stock cars. One of the Kidz needed surgery on his knee, so we got a replacement from Washington, G, a twelve-year-old. He didn't fit in. He wasn't from the 'hood, so D made his life a misery, putting handcuffs on him and dumping him into a garbage can.

What to do with D and R? These kids could definitely be diagnosed as VFC, a condition known to all psychiatrists (very f-ing crazy). For a while, the teachers debated the possibility of expelling them from the school, but we were told that was a no-go. It was in their contract that we had to give them an education. What to do? If we succeeded in expelling them from the classroom, they would hang around, beating on the classroom walls or opening the door, yelling obscenities, and throwing dirt into the room. We knew the pattern. During school hours they needed to be in someone's control or, failing that, under restraint like a crazy old aunt chained in the attic. Maybe we could add them to the elephant line. I can visualize them now, with the chains and stakes driven into the ground – Sabu, Jennie, Congo, Asia, Banana, T and D. How long would it be though before the elephants started complaining?

One day, the suits came back to visit the boys. "We are going to have random drug tests," they were told. "If any of you test positive for drugs, you are out of here."

I leaned over to the teacher at my side. "They'll never do it," I said. "This act is too good. They only test people they want to get rid of. There is nothing they can do that will get them fired, short of screwing the zebras, and actually, they just might get away with that. We are stuck with them."

Toward the end of that tour, a couple of suits came to speak to the teachers. They told us that the next tour would no longer have all the child-centered acts. The Russian kids, the Chinese, the Bulgarians – all these would be returning to their own countries. The circus was only going to keep the Chicago Kidz. That meant that just one teacher would be needed.

"Which one of you would like to continue with us and be the Chicago Kidz' teacher?" they asked.

We all looked at each other and almost in chorus we responded, "I resign."

Well, my time with the circus was over. The tour wound up in December as we returned to Florida. I got a lift back home with Eric, our ringmaster. Eric had his own car. From our final destination in West Florida, he drove me back to my home. My two grown children had been living there, parent-free and rent-free for years. I didn't quite know how to make them aware that the good times were over. Eric handled it for me. He smoothed on his one white glove, the regulation single white glove of a ringmaster. As we entered the house, he trailed one gloved finger across the furniture as if testing for dust. From his expression, they knew that they had failed the test.

It was good to be home, but I was used to the fast lane. What could I do? No more excitement, no more living on the high wire. Life was going to be dull, dull, dull. And so it was – for a while – until eventually I got the phone call. It was from the New York agency. "How would you like to fly out to a Mediterranean island, to work on a movie shoot? It's a movie called *Gladiator*. This sounded too good to be true. "How many kids?" I asked.

"Just one," came the reply.

"And what role does he play in this movie?"

"Oh, he's the heir to the Roman Empire!"

Wow! Another grand adventure on the horizon. I couldn't wait to start. There was a frantic period of preparation. For the next few weeks, I assembled my paperwork – passport, money, tickets, etc. I carefully packed my tropical island wardrobe, pills, and toiletries. Finally the day arrived and I was boarding a plane for Paris where I changed planes and took a flight into Malta. There I was met at the airport and driven straight to my hotel in Valetta.

This was the place that housed most of the cast of the movie. When I pulled my suitcase into the hotel lobby, I noticed a tall, lean young man with a long curving scar down one cheek. He was eyeing me with interest and approached confidently.

With a broad Scottish accent he asked, "Yer the new tutor, ain't ya?"

I was a bit taken aback, but I nodded assent.

"English, ain't ya?" he accused.

Once again I agreed.

"Sheep shaggers, the lot of ya," he pronounced.

I stepped back in shock, then gathered my senses together and glared at him.

"Well, I happen to know why you Scottish men wear kilts." I announced.

"And why's that?" he inquired with interest.

I looked him straight in the eyes.

"'Cause a Scottish sheep can hear a zipper a mile away."

He snorted and laughed. It was great! We smiled happily at each other. It had taken less than five minutes, but we had bonded. We had insulted each other with equanimity. What a great encounter! Tommy was to remain a good friend for the rest of my time in Malta.

I checked in and made it to my room. What a change! No more 7-by-7½ foot minispace. Here I was in a beautiful, deluxe hotel bedroom with a gorgeous bathroom. Could life get any better? Well, yes it could. After settling in I ventured out and met my new colleagues. It wasn't just my student and his mother: it was an amazing collection of the Who's Who of acting.

Anyway, I'll save them for the future.